MAN,

YOU MATTER

By

PASTOR SONYA Y. CHELTENHAM

Printed in the United States of America.

ISBN-13: 978-0-57876545-7
ISBN-10: 0578765457

Cover and Interior Design by: *Designed by Evelyn*
Editorial, proofing, fact-checking, and publishing services provided by: *Carmen the Wordsmith, Hope Christmas Goude,* CarsamontePublishing@gmail.com.
Cover wrap created and designed by: KyleWestproductions@gmail.com.

DEDICATION

I dedicate this book to my loving husband, Ed Cheltenham. Thank you for the tremendous patience, concern and support you have shown in each of my endeavors for the last 45 years of our marriage. I love you more each day!

ACKNOWLEDGEMENTS

Special thanks to my partners in ministry. Your prayers and endless support provide the strength on which I humbly stand.

I also want to acknowledge Carmen Glover (the Wordsmith) for her skills, abilities, guidance, and her gift of encouragement. It is by her hands that I was able to bring this gift forward. Thank you for excellent, compassionate service in helping me birth, edit, proof, and publish this baby. Much appreciation to Hope Christmas-Goude for your keen proofing eye!

Finally, to all those who will read this book, may you come to understand that in the full scheme of things, you truly matter. Maintaining an *"I matter"* mindset is the optimum stance in life! It is not wealth, power nor standing on a grand stage that will propel you forward in life. Rather, it is knowing your value in Christ that will ignite the doors of destiny to swing open on your behalf. After reading this book, it is my desire that you find great comfort in knowing that when you take your final breath, it will be just like inhaling sweet air, knowing that you mattered to at least One!

TABLE OF CONTENTS

INTRODUCTION

I have noticed a few social media posts speaking to the issue of a real man. One was a woman attesting to the fact that she had finally found a "real man." There were lots of hearts and high fives as other women celebrated her find, along with disdain from those who had lost hope of finding someone similar.

As I read through the comments, a nagging question kept rolling through my mind. I tried to dismiss the thought but found myself coming back to the same problem. So, I asked myself again, 'What is a real man?' I decided to ask men and women what makes a real man and what are the deciding factors confirming if they are in the presence of an authentic man.

At the end of the discussion, all I could say was, "Wow! Wow!" to the responses I received from a number of people defining their definition of a real man. I found myself just as confused, with more questions than before. Who was the judge? And what factors were used to reach this conclusion?

The stereotypes used by our society resembles that of Rocky Balboa; a tough stud, with a hard-cut body and six-pack abs, more fitting for a New York billboard. Or a well-manicured Denzel Washington sporting a Brooks Brothers suit with matching tie and shoes. But are these *real men*? Can we measure a *real* man by how much time he has invested in bodybuilding or his collection of beautiful women or fancy suits?

If this is indeed the measure of a real man, no wonder most men feel inadequate, beat down, and left out. Because the truth is, most men do not lift weights, and most cannot afford Brooks Brothers suits. There are other truths: Real men cry. Real men hurt. They can be insecure about their looks, life, and relationships as well. They might lack fatherly figures to show them how to navigate becoming real men in a world that disrespects and emasculates them. They grapple with life, trying to attain the fleeting status of a "real-man". It feels like a dream when they don't have a concrete measurement.

If there was a valid method to measure manhood, wouldn't most men attempt to measure up? So, in my quest to answer some of these questions, I realized when trying to understand a prototype, you go to the manufacturer's operation manual to understand the proper application and use of that item. The progenitor of man is God. Man is His design, His creation, and His dream of those qualified to reign with Him.

God, see's men through a loving Father's eyes. Just consider seeing yourself, your manhood, and your future through God's eyes; your Heavenly Father. A Father who has planned for the whole world to embrace the magnificence of *you!* Ask yourself, '*What can I accomplish if I believed God's design? What could I accomplish if money were not an issue? What could I accomplish if I believed I am God's original design?*' Considering you are the head and not the tail, the beginning vision and not the end thought! When God designed you, He said you were not only good, but "*very good!*"

As I considered my thoughts about who men are in this world, I believe God pricked my heart to feel what they feel. I prayed for men to take their place, stand their ground, and navigate this world; they are designed to do it. It was humbling to discover the obstacles and roadblocks erected in the path of most men. They may include the lack of a father figure, lack of adequate education, lack of consistent opportunities, and let us not overlook the weaponizing of men of color (MOC). These factors and others are the weapons formed against men working to keep them unfaithful, unfruitful, unloving, and unkind; even to themselves.

Men, at this point in your life, you may not feel successful, or you may think your failures are just too great. But I encourage you to be honest with yourself about what brought you to this point. Assess where you are, to plot a course that will bring greatness into your own life. It is the only way to build a future with the hope of leaving a legacy that will not perish for the second and third generations that follow.

So, men hold your heads high! You are redeemed daily and converted to authentic manhood. You are created to be in relationship with God; you will never discover who you are or reach the purpose for your life outside of building a relationship in continuous fellowship with God. All men are different, so never disagree with God on who He created *you* to be by trying to be someone else. Enhance, bless, and build the skin you're in!

You are unique and wonderfully made to become the best expression of *you*. A man is responsible for continuing the knowledge, hope, and passion within. You are to do that by teaching, training, and guiding those under your authority into what you know about God. Real men know they are not ready for a sexual relationship with a woman until they provide leadership and take care of her physical and emotional needs. According to the Bible, real men lay a solid foundation for their future, knowing the sacrifices their goals may present.

Have faith and keep moving, God's got you! Trust your journey because God planned it. You can trust God even when you don't see Him. It takes patience, but it will work to your benefit. Man was purposed to work hard, and the world is designed to work for you, so keep moving! Look for the light of hope on your darkest days, remembering the Lord orders your steps. The biggest mistake in life is to give up, so don't let circumstances and issues destroy you because *you must win.*

When a man seeks to know *he matters*, he begins with God, the journey shines a light and encourages him toward knowing himself better and more intimately. Taking on this process is not a quick fix, but it must begin somewhere. So, you might ask, why begin with *you*? Because, Man, *You* Matter!

CHAPTER ONE

WHAT MATTERS?

"If a man wishes to be sure of the road he treads on, he must close his eyes and walk in the dark."
— St. John of the Cross

For the purpose of this book, to matter is to consider with respect your worth, excellence, usefulness, and importance.

The struggle to determine what matters to each of us invites a journey through the vast ocean of our minds. This journey forces first the discovery of who we are, and what we value. It can be exhausting to push past all the distractions in life; people, careers, family, friends, pleasure, pain, hurt, love, unfulfilled promises and acquiring things, not to mention the violation of your body, soul, and spirit you may have endured. We will discuss this topic at length in a later chapter. It is rare for any of us to know what will matter in the world tomorrow. The important thing is to continually seek to find what we value most. This life-changing event and spiritual awakening is found by digging into the depths of our own hearts for clues hidden within the city of our soul.

> *"At the end of life, what really matters is not what we bought but what we built; not what we got but what we shared; not our competence but our character, and not our success, but our significance. Live a life that matters. Live a life of love".*
> — **Author Unknown**

The world is fickle! The world will love this person, or that group, a new love song, or some obscure drastic fashion. The world will sleep overnight on a street corner to gain a glimpse of a handsome sports or voluptuous video figure. The world will then in no time start hating the same person tomorrow for the slightest mistake, misstep, or life failure. On your journey for personal change and value, you must know you weren't designed to be a cheap imitation of someone else or a copycat of some fantasy figure. When you play that role, you have given into maintaining the fantasy by seeking the approval of an audience that does not have a relationship with you and cannot know the *real* you.

When you give into others and what they expect, you ultimately live for their applause. The ongoing challenge is to come to grips with the knowledge that when you are not true to yourself, you play to an audience that loves the lie, not the truth of who you really are. Your personal truth can only be seen by permission. This permission is called *intimacy* or phonetically speaking, *in-to-me-see!* The time, patience, and talent to see who you really are is only given to those who deserve a clear glimpse of the strength within you. You cannot be seen in a momentary glimpse; passersby need to keep on steppin'! This type of intimacy (*in-to-me-see*) is not sex at all; it is trusting enough to allow someone the time to peel back the layers of your life.

It inevitably may produce tears causing you to be vulnerable to those given permission to see *into you*. The gift of intimacy is only afforded to those who enter into relationship with you, and rightly so! Most men are guarded where this is concerned, and everyone is not worthy or trustworthy enough to be in relationship with you. When you allow yourself to be completely open to anyone and everyone you are left in the rubble of your own hurts, anger, frustrations, and brokenness. The good part is that these negative issues tend to push us toward finding meaning in our lives. But before we can find life's meaning, we need to begin with ourselves and more importantly with our Creator, God.

Hurts, frustrations, and brokenness are distractions. These distractions always demand measurements based on the same value system in their world. Distractors provide us with an array of predetermined demands that hold our thoughts and desires. They frame how we view the world and ourselves and ultimately determine the outcome of our behavior. What we believe is dynamically tied to how we behave! If our belief system and therefore our behaviors are tied to outward distractions, we never have to own our choices or monitor what we do. The danger of living this life while changing your choices to those of outside influencers sends your life journey down the rabbit hole of someone else's whims and schemes. It doesn't matter whether we come to this place on our own or someone else forces us here, those aged-old questions of '*Who am I?*' '*Do I really matter?*' begins to haunt and torment your very existence.

These age-old questions must be faced by us all. It is like the giant that David faced on a hill far away that seemed relentless, intimidating, unyielding and unmanageable. On first thought, this giant poses a three-part question, "Is the ten-foot giant in the room?" *"Can it be ignored?"* *"Should it be ignored?"* Then finally, we must examine ourselves by asking, *"Can I live my life without making these distinctions?"* It would be like existing without the integrity of Shakespeare's words, *"To thine own self be true … Thou canst not then be false to any man."* Finding out what really matters and coming to the realization of how you matter is an invitation to step on the floor of life and dance to the music of your choice.

So, the first thing we learn is that we above all other life forms have the gift of choice. Many may see this gift as a curse because they have settled for a life of mediocrity and mundane existence. Therefore, for this writer to suggest they muster the strength to make a life choice is likened to moving Mt. Everest. However, the power to choose is the ability to see the mountain and decide today for the first time in your life, *"I will stand in front of this mountain and demand that it be removed to the sea!"*

The Journey Begins

The journey begins inside where you travel through the good, the bad, the angry, and the ugly thoughts, experiences, fears, and frustrations you have gone through over the years. What do you remember as a child that replays itself in your adult dream life? Was it the uninvited touch of a groping adult whose violations took life's journey from you, killing the flower of the little girl created to be a queen, or bending the tree inside the little boy created to be a king?

Could it have been the untimely death of a parent, or the absence of a parent, who either left or was too busy nursing a drug or alcohol problem to understand their vital role in your life?

This list is endless, painful, and relentless. These issues expose potholes and pit stops along life's journey that seek to define who you are and if you matter. These weights and hindrances delay you coming to the prearranged appointment, your place of predestined glory. The hills and valleys of failed marriages, failed businesses, and failed ventures attempt to undermine who you are and what you were designed and destined to do. The residue of having to walk through the Valley of the Shadow of Death presents itself in every area of your life. If you have not come to the plateau of accepting what's been missing in your life, you are replaying these devastating events over and over again. Your mind is a great tool; it works to your advantage and unfortunately to your disadvantage.

The mind can record everything good and bad, which means it also can replay events experienced throughout your day and your life. The traumas tend to be high on the rerun movie guide of your mind. These violations and traumas are constantly invading your dream life on a daily or nightly basis. These traumas act as invaders of your rest, peace, and sweet sleep, framing who you are, as they push you into accepting the lifestyle of a victim. It has been said many times, "Free your mind and your body will follow," or something like that. It is very true that if we were able, like a computer, to delete or erase the hindering issues of our mind, we could free-up space for better, lasting and beneficial memories. Many studies have gone to great lengths to show the relationship between mental health and physical health. It is interesting to learn that by going through depression or feeling low, or having the blues has in many cases been followed by a physical illness. It is true that how we feel in our life and how we feel about our life will have a drastic impact on how well our bodies operate and how healthy they are over time. The Bible says, *"As (a man) thinks in his heart, so is he!"* (Proverbs 23:7, *New King James Version, NKJV*) In other words, what you think in your mind and believe in your heart is inevitably what you will become. Therefore, taking care of your mind and your body is God's greatest desire for you. God says in 3 John 1:2, *"I desire that you prosper and be in good health even as your soul (mind) prospers."* God is indicating in this passage that a prosperous mind (soul) is in direct alignment with good health. Even scientists have traced the emotional responses of the brain to the quality and value we place on our lives. If we give into the stressors of life and continue living with a damaged belief system, it pushes us into a place in our minds that emotionally support the belief that "We *REALLY* Don't Matter." I was reading *Life Journal,* and the writer made note of the mind, emotion, and body/health connection. It stated, *"In a very simplified way, an emotion starts with an emotional stimulus being received by a sense organ. This information is relayed to the limbic system, which is the brain's very domineering emotional processing area. It is located centrally in the brain, connects to most other brain areas and many body parts and regulates chemicals that affect how the entire brain operates."* (Dr. Joseph E. LeDoux, 2002) This process keeps us locked in a place of being devalued to the point of not believing we really matter to anyone, and therefore, we don't matter to ourselves. The problem with this train of thought is that we have still failed to measure our worth or value by the One Who formed, designed, and created us.

> *"My friend, I ask, 'Who do you think you are to question God? Does the clay have the right to ask the potter why he shaped it the way he did?'"* *(Romans 9:20,*
> — *Contemporary English Version, CEV)*

We must admit to ourselves that on many occasions, we questioned what God had in mind when He created us. It is especially hard and upsetting when people, by their look and stares, co-sign with what we are questioning God about. "I'm not pretty. I'm not handsome. I'm too fat. I'm way too thin. I'm not strong and virile. My hair is too short. My hair is ugly. My skin is too dark. My skin is too light. Others are better looking. They have more money and are more intelligent than I am!" Maybe you have said these things, and more, silently to yourself. But what if God had asked us, 'How should I make you? What shape will suit you?' We would find a multitude of people to use as examples of how we believe we should look, be and feel! "I want Halle Berry's face. I want Denzel Washington's smile, Beyoncé's body, or hair; The Rock's body, Sofia Loren's sex appeal, Oprah's business savvy," and on and on in your attempt to shape the perfect you. What you are ultimately telling God is that you don't like His choices and He made a huge mistake with making us. The result is that God didn't ask and since He is the only one who can see your future, He knows the best design for you! He knew what your choices and those of others close to you would be and how they would affect you. He knew that things in your life would be difficult at best, but He created you to take a lickin' and keep on tickin'!! So, as you take this journey, make your first step to accepting you for who God created you to be, and more importantly, who you were created to become. It is your future God wants to usher you into, although He knows your past must be settled, faced, and healed to get you to your destiny. Remember, God doesn't make mistakes and He created you to add beauty and strength to His garden as only you can.

Receive the Gift of you!

"It was by Him that everything was created: the heavens, the earth, all things within and upon them, all things seen and unseen, thrones and dominions, spiritual powers and authorities. Every detail was crafted through His design, by His own hands, and for his purposes."
— (Colossians 1:16, The Voice, VOICE)

God has crafted, carved, molded, and made each of us uniquely according to His design with His own hands. He did it for His reasons, purposes and for His specific pleasure. With passionate love and determination, He designed your distinguishing features. Your look, hair and eye color, your height and skin color, your body shape and structure were predetermined in the counsel of His own mind. He did not ask anyone how you should look or what your distinguishing characteristics should be; however, He designed you to bring individual, unique beauty and strength to your destiny and His purposes. God was so careful in your design, meticulous in His thoughts toward you that He planned who your parents would be. They may not have planned for you; it may have been a huge surprise, but God planned every inch of you! Every curve, every pound, every nuance of the unique you. He planned, mixed, called into being and brought together the correct DNA to produce the magnificent you. It is true that parents do not plan most children, and painfully I admit I'm one of them, but all children are in God's plans. Since God is timeless, He can see all the events and issues of life at the same time, past, present, and future. God considered all the issues and hardships that may occur in your life and He built you to last. God has a master plan for everything and all things. There is nothing that exists by accident or mistake. God put all things into motion, and they live and have their being by His design and His handiwork.

You may ask why would a God like Him do all of this for you? John 3:16 explains it like this, *"For God so loved the world that he gave his only begotten son, that whosoever believes in him should not perish but have everlasting life" (paraphrased). The Voice Bible states, "For God expressed His love for the world in this way: He gave His only Son so that whoever believes in Him will not face everlasting destruction, but will have everlasting life."* Here's the point. God didn't send His Son into the world to judge it; instead, He is here to rescue a world headed toward certain destruction.

God, in His infinite wisdom, did all of this for you and will continue to do wonderful things through you because He loves you. He simply loves you, because in you He sees His design and His creation that He yearns to be in fellowship with. God loves you so much that He has given His very best, His only, and His all, which is His son Jesus Christ, as a love offering in your place. Since God is the full expression of love in all that He may say and do, it is His pleasure to express this love to you, His creation. You have been blessed and chosen to receive God's immeasurable, immutable love. You don't have to pay for it or do anything to gain it, just accept it through His son Jesus Christ. When you make God the center of your life, everything good and perfect will be realized by you because you are that special to God. Many people struggle with finding their place and purpose in life. They take many paths to locate that sweet spot but miss the mark because they begin their journey with trying to discover themselves. I have heard many people say they were trying to find themselves and they set out on personal journeys. These journeys are taken through physical travel exploring one city, one town, one state, and country after another. Or they may use mental exploration through the vehicles of meditation or some other metaphysical means of attempting to find themselves, believing if they accomplish that task, they will also find purpose. No one wants to live without purpose. Living without purpose is like having an empty longing for our lives to have meaning. Most folks desire to live a life so that their choices and actions impact others positively.

There are many reasons why people are lost and seeking purpose in empty directions. When the answer to our search is everything, and it is tied to absolutely everything about our lives, the search pushes us to know that everything begins with God. If you are seeking purpose for your life or with your life, don't waste your journey, whether physical or mental, in empty stops. Begin by pursuing the God Who's pursuing you. He is pulling at your heartstrings even now, trying to bring you into His outstretched arms and His all-encompassing love. Won't you begin this journey of realizing how much you Matter with Him (Jesus Christ)? It doesn't matter what others say or think about you; it only matters what He says about you! Only His words have the power to change your life! So, look to His Word (The Bible) where you will find everything you need to become successful in your quest of just wanting to matter.

Once your relationship with Christ begins, by simply asking Him to come into your life and by you accepting His glorious Salvation, you are now ready to explore and learn from God's Basic Instructions Book (Bible). In it you will find the road map to your purpose and evidence that you positively matter! Using God's Instruction Book, you will find how fearfully and wonderfully you were designed, and that you are a one-of-a-kind Designer's original. You will also learn that God has a specific purpose for you that only you can complete. By completing this study, you will find peace that surpasses understanding and love overflowing. Finally, you will learn that you are the answer to someone's prayer. What are you waiting for? The thing you have dreamed about, your search, begins here.

CHAPTER TWO

CUT AND MOLDED INTO THE MAN I AM

Time to make that change!

"Now let's search out our thoughts and ways and return to the Eternal"
— (Lamentations 3:40, VOICE)

———————— ༄ ༄ ༄ ————————

Most of the time, we spend our lives trying to change our circumstances and people around us. We struggle to change our looks by changing the color of our hair with dye or the color of our eyes with lenses, building bigger muscles or chasing that six pack. Some have used surgery to change their appearance making their noses larger or smaller, raising their cheek bones or removing wrinkles, attempting to change the outer covering forgetting their problem is an internal issue. We are not our issues; we are not what people have determined us to be, and we are not our labels either.

We are more than the broken pieces we have come to accept. We are not the fractured image reflected in mirrors or what's reflected in the eyes or comments of others. By moving to change how we see ourselves, we will in turn alter how we see others and therefore the world. This change will challenge us to lay down the weight of issues plaguing our lives for years. These can be feelings of inadequacy, feeling you don't measure up, or that everyone is better than you. It also includes low self-worth, covered wounds, unhandled hurts, denial, anger, and a victim spirit. Over the next chapters, we will explore these and other issues at length taking the time to confront the issues that cause us to believe we don't matter. Most of what will be discovered through this change will take faith to lay aside the weight that so easily overcomes us.

> *"Since we stand surrounded by all those who have gone before, an enormous cloud of witnesses, let us drop every extra weight, every sin that clings to us and slackens our pace, and let us run with endurance the long race set before us."*
> *— (Hebrews 12:1, 2, Voice)*

You must begin the work with asking the Lord Jesus Christ into your heart to be your personal Savior. He will do that, and He will walk you through this process of renewal as you learn to accept you and love you as God, Himself does. Our thoughts and feelings sit with our egos; some have an overly-inflated ego while others harbor a deflated ego. In both instances, they have received tainted information regarding their self-worth and have consequently developed a bound ego. In life, a bound ego presents itself with a prideful view of yourself or a self-debasing view. These feelings frame how we approach life and how we see ourselves in the world.

A bound ego will grow into a victimized spirit where it appears everyone is either doing things to us or keeping us from those things that are rightfully ours. In both cases, deliverance must be sought and received to walk in the freedom we inherited from becoming a child of God. It is your birthright! Also, not unlike most royals, you didn't *join* in; you were *born* in the lineage of Jesus Christ which gives you the blood type to receive the complete inheritance listed in His "Will and (Old & New) Testaments," (The Bible). It is waiting for you to claim it. Change is more than a desire or a good thing to say; real change takes work and determination. You must be willing to fight the internal argument that constantly tries to stop your forward progress. Change is gained in baby steps and a daily struggle with your own inner voices, the voices that echo the words and deeds that are responsible for you feeling like a victim. Real change, lasting change, the spirit-building kind of change, only comes when the victim spirit is brought into subjection to the Holy Spirit. Now, let's look at the different types of victim spirits we sometimes must deal with. Some of you have been wrestling with these spirits for so long, you think they are you. But we must do the work to recognize, acknowledge and put a stop to the areas of our chosen retreat where we ourselves become the victim. Then we will be able to overcome these spirits and resist them until they flee from our lives.

The Victimized Spirit

"On Your behalf, our lives are endangered constantly; we are like sheep awaiting slaughter. But no matter what comes, we will always taste victory through Him who loved us."
— *Romans 8:36, 37*

(All of these victim illustrations are new! Format is the same circumstances different)

Victimized by Family: We must also understand that there were victims during Biblical times. They were probably more prevalent than we realize for both men and women because there were no laws of punishment except the unspoken rule of families and tribes. Joseph was a kid who was victimized by his family. Joseph was an up-and-coming young man. He was one of twelve sons born to his father, Jacob. It was clear to his other brothers that their dad loved Joseph more than he did them. It was because Jacob was an old man when Joseph was born, and Joseph was born to his father's favorite wife, Rachel! So, he was very proud that he could have another son at an old age.

Life at home for Joseph was not unlike other large families today, especially when there are all boys in the home. The difference is, the usual horseplay and fun of brothers in a large family wasn't the same fun and games for Joseph and his brothers. His brothers didn't just struggle with him for their father's affection. They grew to literally hate Joseph because of the special treatment their father gave to him. To make things worse, Joseph wanted to share his dreams and proclamations, insisting he would be someone great and rule over them when he grew up! Everyone who met Joseph knew he was full of promise, and to further upset his brothers, their father gave him a special jacket with magnificent colors. Joseph's dreams were great and audacious; he loved sharing them with his brothers or anyone willing to listen. These dreams were of Joseph becoming great in their country, so great he would rule over his family. So, Joseph's relationship with his brothers was increasingly becoming hostile.

Joseph's brothers hated him so much they rejected him, left him in a pit plotting to kill him. One morning, Joseph was home with their father while his brothers tended the sheep. They were gone so long Jacob sent Joseph to find his brothers because he was worried about them. Joseph went to find his brothers and ran into a man that told him where they were. Joseph searched in that direction and found his brothers. They too saw Joseph coming from far away because he was wearing the coat of many colors their father gave him. Their jealousy became intense as he approached them. They didn't wait for Joseph to tell them what their father said, instead, they threw him into a nearby pit, planning to leave him there. But his brother Reuben, who really didn't want to hurt him, had planned to come back later, pull him out and take him home unharmed.

When Reuben returned, Joseph was nowhere to be found. Reuben did not know that his brothers came back before him, taking their brother and selling him into slavery to merchants headed to Egypt. Joseph's brothers knew they had to tell their father something. So, they took Joseph's coat of many colors and dipped it into goat's blood and told their father that a wild animal had killed him. Eventually, these merchants sold Joseph to rich politicians, Potiphar and his wife. Potiphar was the chief officer of Pharaoh's guard. Soon Potiphar noticed there was something special about Joseph. He saw his abilities and that he was no common slave, so Potiphar put Joseph over all his other slaves, soon placing him over his entire house. It wasn't long before Joseph's influence and leadership caused Potiphar's home to prosper.

While working in Potiphar's house, Joseph encountered everyone in the house including Potiphar's wife Zelicha, and her friends. Joseph was strong, good-looking, and these women enjoyed watching him work. One evening, there was a block party, and everyone was outside enjoying the food and fun, except Joseph. The festivals were usually given for Egyptian gods and Joseph didn't choose to attend. Zelicha knew he would be at home alone and she made an excuse to stay home, too. Zelicha was a beautiful woman and she just knew he would be attracted to her. Zelicha threw herself at him and promised him many things. But Joseph held onto his integrity and ran from the house as she was pulling his coat that he had to leave behind. After the festival, to cover her tracks with Joseph running away, Zelicha lied and said he tried to rape her.

Although Potiphar knew that Joseph was above suspicion and could never be guilty of such a crime, he had to uphold the honor of his wife. He had Joseph tortured, beaten, and thrown into prison. Joseph had to be second-guessing what he believed about himself. Life's trials and issues can kill a dream if you let it! There he was, the kid with the big dreams, sitting in prison on a trumped-up charge! Joseph never lost heart, and as destiny would have it, he ran into the king's butler and baker who were in prison because they did not please the king. The three men spent time in prison talking with each other to pass the long days. One day as Joseph looked for them to have their usual conversation to pass the time, he found them both looking down and upset. He thought it was just being in prison, which has a way of making you feel as if you don't matter. He asked them what was up. Why were they so low? They answered, "We both had dreams that bothered us because there was no one that could interpret them." Joseph explained to them that he believed in God and God is the One that gives meaning to dreams. However, if they wanted to tell him the dreams, he would pray and ask God to help him understand their meanings. They agreed, so the chief butler gave the details of his dream first, stating, "In my dream, out of nowhere a vine was in front of me, and on the vine were three branches. They were all budding, and right away they blossomed, and the clusters became ripe grapes before my eyes.

I had Pharaoh's cup in my hand, and I took the grapes, pressed them into Pharaoh's cup, and I gave the cup to him." Joseph prayed and told the chief butler, "This is what your dream means. The three branches are three days and within three days, Pharaoh will release you from prison and restore you to your position, and you will put Pharaoh's cup in his hand, just as you used to do when you were his cupbearer. That's what your dream means. However, I need to remember how I helped you with your dream, and when you are out, when all goes well with you, remember me and show me kindness by mentioning me to Pharaoh and get me out of this prison. I was forcibly carried off from the land of the Hebrews, and even here, I have done nothing to deserve being put in a dungeon."

The baker saw that Joseph's explanation of the dream was good, so he said to him, "I also had a dream. I dreamed there were three bread baskets on my head and in the top basket were all kinds of baked food for the king, but the birds were eating the food out of the basket on my head." Joseph said, "Ok, this is what the dream means. The three baskets stand for three days and before the end of three days, the king will cut off your head! He will hang your body on a pole, and the birds will eat your flesh." Three days later, on his birthday, the king gave a feast for all his officers. In front of his officers, he released from prison the chief butler who served his wine and the chief baker, just as Joseph had said. The chief baker did not keep his word when he was free; he forgot all about Joseph. It seems that Joseph will remain a victim of family abuse and circumstances. But his dream described his destiny and it was still going to be fulfilled. (Taken from Genesis 40:10-23, paraphrased) Joseph ended up spending several years in prison waiting for his destiny to come to life! He reminded himself often that dreams delayed are not dreams denied! Have faith!

During Joseph's prison term, he became a trustee over other prisoners because when you're chosen, you always rise to the top. Finally, Joseph, an innocent man, was brought out of prison because one night, the king had a disturbing dream that he couldn't find anyone to interpret. Isn't it strange how others may know what you know but when it's your turn, no one can take your place? Joseph was successful in helping the king. The king's dream was strategic in putting Joseph in the right place at the right time. The king got his answer on how to help his nation; Joseph was given a position of power in that plan; he received great honors and was able to execute the plan God gave through the king's dream! Was Joseph a victim? I don't think so!

New story

Victim of Hopelessness: In 2006, the story of Chris Gardner was a hit movie called *The Pursuit of Happyness*, in which his character was played by Will Smith. Chris is an African American man born under similar circumstances of many African-American men in the U.S., perhaps the world. He was born on February 9, 1954 to Thomas Turner and Bettye Jean. Chris's mom had a daughter, Ophelia, from her first marriage, before she met Thomas Turner. Chris's father left the family and wasn't present most of Chris's life. He only saw his father twice in his lifetime. Chris did not grow up interacting with a dad and he doesn't remember his father at any childhood events. The absence of a strong man in the life of a growing boy can cause future issues and a sense of hopelessness. It is difficult to impossible to become what you have not seen modeled in front of you. The two times he saw his father was when Chris was 28 years old when they crossed paths and at his father's funeral. To make matters worse for Chris, a few years later his mother married Freddie Triplett. She had two daughters with Freddie, Chris's stepsisters, Sharon, and Kimberly. His mother marrying Freddie Triplett was one of the worst things that could have happened to Chris. It invited a level of misery that he never thought possible. Freddie Triplett was a brutal and abusive man, both physically and verbally.

He would hit and physically harm Chris. He would put a gun in his face and tell him he wasn't his father, which further assaulted his sense of safety, security, and manhood. When Freddie was angry with Chris, he would grab him and put him out of their house, even as a young teen. One night, around Christmas, he put him out in the streets, and Chris had to live outside which caused him to hang with rough guys, gang members, and to use drugs. Chris was eventually put in the foster care system and stayed in several places. As a grown man, he married Sherry Dyson but was unfaithful to her and had a son with the other woman, Jackie Medina. Chris divorced his wife and began staying with Jackie, who was carrying his child. They eventually married and in 1981 his son Christopher Gardner Jr. was born the same year. At the time, Chris was working in a laboratory as a lab assistant at a college campus in San Francisco.

His job in the lab did not pay enough money to support his family. Chris, trying all he could to change his family's financial situation, decided to become a medical-equipment salesman. Chris struggled at this job too, but he had an inner determination to keep trying and to keep struggling to live a better life. As hard as he tried to make a living, even lugging medical equipment on foot to try to convince doctors and clinics to buy, it still wasn't enough to pay his bills and keep his family with food and housing. The stress of not having enough, and because he wasn't able to help his new wife and the mother of his child, she put him out. This was an awful time for Chris; he was left without enough money to take care of himself. As his life seemed to be going for Chris at this time, he became homeless and was arrested. When he was released from jail, Chris was able to talk his wife into allowing him to come live with her again, and she allowed him to come back. But things didn't work out causing them to file for a divorce. Chris loved his son and would not allow his wife to take him! In anger, she left them.

Without income, Chris and his small son eventually ended up homeless. Chris found himself homeless with a small child, leaving him with very few options other than to live in shelters with his son. But God had a plan, and as destiny would have it, he ran into a man with a red Ferrari on the street and asked, "What do you do?" Gardner really did this. He approached a stockbroker in a parking garage while his son was still an infant. This man decided to help Chris, so he followed up with Chris inviting him for lunch to explain the basics of Wall Street. This is the power to gain wealth, the blessing of opportunity! Because of that one conversation, his life changed forever.

Chris got his first break from Dean Witter, the financial firm, when he applied for an internship they sponsored. He arrived at this interview dressed inappropriately because of his recent release from jail, and staying at a cousin's house where his only clothing was old jeans, a wind breaker and tennis shoes with paint spots on them. But he showed-up! Sometimes just showing up is the best a man can do! He aced his interview and was hired as an intern where he was paid $1000 per month. For Chris, that was a crack in the door toward his dream. He could start holding his head up when he began to provide for his son, no longer sleeping on the streets! Is Chris Gardner a victim? No, I don't think so; he is a man that *MATTERS*! (Gardner 2020)

Victim of Hopeless Circumstances: The Bible tells us about a man named David who, for the most part, was invisible and the least likely one to be picked or chosen by his family or his community, least of all his world. He was a little shepherd boy, one of the sons of Jesse. He had the lowest job in his family, and the lowest in his community. His job and status caused him to spend most of his days and nights alone. You see, being a shepherd boy wasn't the type of job or person most girls wanted to hang around. It could have been how dirty he became from being in the fields, or the smell of sheep that became impossible for him to get off his clothes, not to mention his skin. Being in the sun every day gave his skin a red leather look so that most folks called him "Ruddy Red." David was such a loner that most folks didn't know he was one of Jesse's sons. David's life had to be frustrating because he lived in the shadows of his brothers and as a second thought of his father.

As David's life progressed, he was hunted by the men in power of the land, who hated him because God had spoken purpose into his life when he was just a lowly shepherd boy. David's life seems to be a continuous round of struggle, war, and frustration. He was a man prone to bad decisions, like taking one of his soldier's wives as his own. He allowed his lustful nature to get the best of him after watching her bathe on her balcony in the evenings. He also struggled with lying about his issues so he would concoct elaborate stories to cover his bad decisions, like the night he noticed Bathsheba bathing in the open air of her rooftop, as was the custom of his day. He was so overwhelmed by her beauty, the dark brown color of her skin, the water dripping off her voluptuous curves like honey off a rock.

Everything stood still while he watched as she rested in the warmth of her bath and in the warmer desert night air. Bathsheba never noticed David the King, the most powerful man in the land, watching her so intently that he couldn't walk away. David allowed his lust to lead him and he used his power to demand her presence. His one sinful act morphed into a lifetime of lies, deception, and murder, because Bathsheba became pregnant. David tried to hide his voyeurism and sexual act from Bathsheba's military husband. The lie was for Bathsheba's husband, Uriah to come home from war and sleep with his wife which would cause him to think her pregnancy was from him. But Uriah was a dedicated soldier; he refused to enjoy the comfort of his wife while his men fought the war. So, Uriah opted to return to battle, which turned David's lie into premeditated murder.

David, being the king, had the power to decide what part of the war Uriah would return to, so he sent word for him to be put on the frontlines and Uriah was killed. Since Bathsheba was carrying his child, he took her as one of his wives. Although David made terrible decisions, he loved God and pursued him passionately. This was David's strength; in all his doings and ways he acknowledged God as his source, and he was quick to repent. The Bible indicates David was very courageous, and he fought strong in battle. Even as a young man he would slaughter beasts with his bare hands that came to eat his sheep. God honored David because of his open heart and his love for Him. He knew David's weakness with committing adultery. God knew David was guilty of murder, and of openly disobeying Him! But when he came to himself, David didn't fool around with empty words like, "I'm sorry."

He would fall on his face and beg God to forgive him and if that wasn't enough, he would tear his clothes off and sit for days in sackcloth and ashes, the itchiest combination you can inflict on yourself. David had other flaws. He was an absent father, failing to discipline his children to honor and obey God and the laws of the land. David's life teaches us that we must be honest with ourselves, others and especially God by a willingness to repent from all wrong doings. We must also know that even though God offers forgiveness for everything we do, He will not always dismiss the consequences of the bad decisions we make. God values our faith in Him and deals with us according to our faith. Despite life's ups and downs, the Lord is ever-present to give us comfort and help. Was David a victim? No, I don't think so! He was a man that MATTERED!

THE HOPELESS VICTIM

LeBron Raymone James Sr. was born December 30, 1984 in Akron, Ohio. At the time of his birth, his mother, Gloria Marie James, was only sixteen years old. LeBron's father is Anthony McClelland, who has been convicted of many crimes and was never interested in being part of LeBron's life. He was an absent parent leaving Gloria with few choices with raising her son on her own. LeBron and his mother struggled to survive, not having enough for the bare necessities until they met Frank Walker and his family. Frank seeing that LeBron not only had athletic abilities, he was especially gifted in basketball and he allowed LeBron to play on his team with his son. After moving often and being hungry often, Gloria finally allowed LeBron to live with Frank and his family. LeBron's mom wanted him to have a life she couldn't afford to give him. While living with the Walker family, LeBron continued to excel at basketball. He played in the Amateur Athletic Union (AAU) while a youth and attended an all-white private school for his high school years. LeBron was drafted into the NBA at 19 years old making him the youngest on the Olympic squad. Since that time, he has gained great success despite his childhood. Is LeBron a victim? No, I don't think so. He is a man that MATTERS. (Britannica n.d.)

There are many stressors that come into play when making life decisions. When we are faced with life decisions big or small, most of us do our best to make good decisions. Many times, despite our good intentions, we make poor choices. These choices are reflected in the people we hang around, the jobs we take or quit, how we spend money and ultimately how we treat our bodies. Choices for most folks, regardless of what their needs, may be difficult in the best of situations because the greater the stress in deciding, the greater the setup for failure.

When the decision is going to bring us immediate gratification over our perceived need, we are more likely to choose poorly. It has been determined that most of us have such a high fear of failure that it greatly affects our decision-making ability to the point we end up making a decision we regret. Scientists indicate that when we make decisions we regret, it influences our future brain activity. Our brains don't forget the bad decisions we made. They become hardwired in our minds and our brains keep emotional memories of these experiences. Our minds then use these experiences to influence and shape our future decisions. Many studies have shown that the end of an experience, whether it's good or bad, has greater influence on your future choices than the overall experience itself. Most everyone has a tendency to choose immediate gratification, even if it equates to a poor choice. However, even amid living out our choices we never lose the power to make sound choices that change our direction and our destiny.

THE VICTIM OF POOR CHOICES

There was a young woman who was raised in a pretty good family. They tried to do what was right, as well as raise her and her siblings doing what was right for themselves and others. When people spoke of this young woman she was labeled by her choice of profession. I'm sure she didn't grow up with this profession as her personal choice, but life has a way of presenting us with choices that immediately gratify our needs and desires or the needs and desires of others. This young woman had that mystical look, dark olive skin, long black wavy hair, and deep black coffee brown eyes. The contrast of her hair and skin caused her eyes to sparkle and pulled most men to watch her walk by. She was headstrong usually, making her own decisions. Rahab was her name, which seems from birth her name described her destiny. The first part of her name "Ra" was the name of an Egyptian god. When put together with the latter half "hab," her name meant insolence or fierceness. Fierceness describes the trait Rahab would need to make a difficult choice that would change her destiny forever.

Rahab was an Amorite and her people served a pantheon of gods. One of the Amorite gods was the god of fertility, where prostitution was encouraged and often utilized in the temple in reference to this god. Rahab was one such woman and was named as a harlot in everything written about her. Rahab's home was on the outskirts of the city, so men could easily come to her home without being seen. Her home was so far off the beaten path that it seemed to be part of the wall that enclosed her city. Rahab was an outgoing woman who knew how to take care of herself. Scripture states she also ran a reputable business of drying flax on her roof top that she dyed red and other beautiful colors, and she sold her items to local women for linen. Her family resided in the city and although they knew of her profession, they loved each other very much. Rahab lived her life believing prostitution was her never-ending story she would have to live out forever. In her mind, she would always be here; it was her self-proclaimed destiny.

She believed there was nothing greater for her, no knight in shining armor, no man marching in to save her from this life of despair and disappointment. She was convinced in her own mind that she had to willingly give herself to men who could never love her, who didn't see her, nor did they regard her as someone who mattered. All of Rahab's men would quickly finish their self-gratifying deeds while leaving her a few pieces of silver on the floor. But these acts always left her lifeless because she participated in the acts of love without the real benefits of love. How could her life be this way? Rahab watched other women her age achieve so much more in their lives and they seemed to matter to everyone around them. While measuring her life, it all equaled to the fact that she should have been further along than this! She should be doing better than this. Isn't this the same place she was in last year? she thought. Fine clothes and better things didn't make her feel any better than they do you.

More expensive cars, or the latest gadgets, the newest cell phone that's made longer, bigger or wider did not change your perception of yourself. Rahab, like many of you, hated her life and therefore she hated herself. Rahab envisioned her life differently. She saw herself better situated, hoped, and dreamed for something better, someone better who had the power to change her life. Then out of the midst of her dreams, it happened on the edge of her hopes. Out of nowhere and everywhere, the God who stood above all the gods Rahab learned to serve, was about to make a move on behalf of His people which would also flood the hopes and dreams of this harlot. The word of these chosen people who were headed to take the land promised to them by storm. They were like locusts but believed like giants.

They looked like ants but fought like trees! There was no stopping them! The thought of these unknown people from a faraway place, slaves who dreamed of a freedom that flowed with milk and honey. All the excitement caused Rahab to think, Those are the people I want to be with; those who can take a licking and keep on ticking; those who get knocked down but get back up. So, Rahab waited with the fierceness of her name for the moment, the right time to make the right choice that would rearrange the DNA of her destiny. It was a normal day and a usual night with familiar visitors who paid for her attention and touch. But this night seemed different. It wasn't the wind; it wasn't the rising of the moon that shined so bright on this night that caused the butterflies in Rahab's belly, it was the anticipation and the jitters that something wonderful was about to happen. Rahab heard footsteps on her rooftop. This wasn't unusual since the back wall of her house was connected to the wall of the city. There was a ramp walkway affixed to the wall so that the guards could walk the perimeter of the city. But tonight, with great anticipation she peeked out her window and saw two men, strangers.

Rahab could tell they were strangers because they dressed and looked different. She knew they were spies sent by their God to take her City. Rahab made a slight noise to get their attention, beckoning them to come to her window. She pulled back the curtains and allowed these two strangers to come and hide in her home. While they were in Rahab's house, they shared the details of their exodus from Egypt and how their God parted the Red Sea and they walked on dry ground. They gave Rahab chills as they described how a group of people who never felt like conquers overthrew the cities of Sihon and Og. Here were two men who were very different from all the other strangers who sought her company and came into her home seeking her favors. These men came seeking nothing, but she knew they had the ability to ask their God to do a favor for her and her family. She also knew that sooner or later the king of Jericho would find out she was hiding spies.

These were men of God on a mission, moving with passion to overthrow the enemies of their God; a God who skillfully set in motion the meeting of a harlot to complete His plan. (Joshua 2) God didn't wait for her to get herself together, or to become respectable; He had called her just like He called you while you were still dirty and doing your thang! God wants you to do something courageous, to walk into your predetermined destiny. Scripture says Rahab the harlot married Salmon a prince of Judah and became a descendant of God's son, Jesus Christ. Scripture says that Rahab helped the spies to leave her city safely and they promised her that when they returned with their army, she and her family would be saved alive. Rahab lived a life plagued with poor choices and decisions. She had resigned herself to that way of life, but God intercepted her journey of destruction and turned her around to a journey of destiny. Rahab made her mark in life and in history which made her so significant to the world that she matters, because she ushered the world's Savior into this life! (Matthew 1:5, 6)

Was Rahab a victim? I don't think so! Rahab was a woman who mattered!

CHAPTER THREE

VICTIM? I DON'T THINK SO!

"You see, God did not give us a cowardly spirit but
a powerful, loving, and disciplined spirit."
— (2 Timothy 1:7, VOICE)

Most victims have become intimidated with either actual or perceived issues, pressures, or problems. Although most of us can attest to becoming victims in many crises, we choose not to make that mindset our home. When we choose to exist in a position of less-than where people, situations and circumstances cause us to be stagnant in growth, hope, power, and love, we are living the life of a victim. Many victims can explain why it's ok for them to live in a wrong situation, and why they must stay in a situation where they are always the victim. Then there are those who have spiritualized their victimization explaining that God needs someone to model suffering with Christ. However, the Scripture indicates that God has not given us a fearful spirit,

and since He is the One that gives us our spirit, He has named that spirit as powerful, loving and disciplined. One translation says, *"God has not given us the spirit of fear but of power, love and a sound mind."* (2 Timothy 1:7)

In my counseling of couples, I have seen battered wives who easily explain away being hit, kicked, and punched. They adamantly proclaim it was only one time, and either they are in denial or they have forced themselves to believe what they are saying in order to survive the constant victimization. I have talked with men who allow their wives to disrespect and dishonor them repeatedly. Other wives and husbands admit the abuse but indicate they must stay because of their great love for him or his great love for her. Some men don't feel worthy of a woman with her beauty or how she makes them feel, so they stay. Finally, most of them resort to blaming all kinds of outside factors for their victimizations. Their excuses range from the spouse having a bad day at work or getting into a fight with the boss. The hardest case is when the spouses explain their behavior by something they did to cause a bad reaction from the other spouse, which is echoing what was said during the beating or verbal putdowns. These examples are the attempts of victims to rationalize and maybe to justify their situation convincing themselves and maybe others that they should remain in a situation that harms them mentally, physically and spiritually.

In these situations, it is not just the bruises, broken bones, or black eyes that linger in healing. It is more so the bruises, broken bones and black eyes of the mind and spirit that can take years or decades to heal if not treated with the balm of the Word. When a person has given into the victim spirit, it is hard if not impossible to face the truth about their situation. Instead, it is far easier to live in the undisciplined world of being a victim. There are children who have fallen victim to a bullying sibling that the parents failed to protect and set boundaries. There are those victimized at work by an overbearing employer who are feeling stuck due to needing the work to pay their bills. These victims will allow the unjust boss to pay them less and abuse them explaining that they need to stay to show their non-Christian boss the love of Christ. Some have been raised by parents who have a victim mindset who spend countless hours explaining away why it's right for them to suffer, and why things always seem to be wrong. They say that the reason they never win is because it builds godly character and strength. Even in a church setting, victims will stay under an abusive pastor or spiritual leader because they have been taught that to be submissive to their leaders is one of God's requirements. These are a few examples of the basic victim mindset that we must challenge and change to understand the depth of how much you matter.

It is often true that those living with a victim mindset usually assume the worst and may even cause problems or issues to ensure the worst is realized. Whenever we begin to agree or cosign with untruths, we bring our spirit in alignment with the enemy, the father of lies, the devil. It gives him permission to further victimize us and to create circumstances where the lie appears true. The believing victim gives power and strength to the lies perpetuated by the enemy. The victim begins the healing process by denouncing the lie they have lived with for so long, and then replacing that stinking thinking with the power of the Word. It is not a one-time event. It takes practice to change and exchange old victimized habits, bound demeaning thoughts and deadly dead-end attitudes with the power of God's Word. This coupled with the presence of the Fruit of the Spirit and the discipline of a sound mind. Recover you must! And fight! YES, you have to!

Let's look at each of these empowering replacement strategies. You must begin to believe that the Word of God has the power to change your entire life. As you look at these Scriptures, don't just read them but memorize them. Then read them often until they become part of your spirit. Commit to concentrating on one Scripture daily for 21 days before moving on to the next one.

THE POWER OF GOD'S WORD

"God means what he says. What he says goes. His powerful Word is sharp as a surgeon's scalpel, cutting through everything, whether doubt or defense, laying us open to listen and obey. Nothing and no one is impervious to God's Word. We can't get away from it—no matter what."
— (Hebrews 4:12, MSG)

"Consequently, faith comes from hearing the message, and the message is heard through the word about Christ."
— (Romans 10:17, NIV)

"When your words came, I ate them;
they were my joy and my heart's delight,
for I bear your name,
Lord God Almighty."
— (Jeremiah 15:16, NIV)

> *"For everything the flesh desires goes against the Spirit, and everything the Spirit desires goes against the flesh. There is a constant battle raging between them that prevents you from doing the good you want to do."*
> — *(Galatians 5:17, VOICE)*
>
> *"Sanctify them in the truth; your word is truth."*
> — *(John 17:17, English Standard Version, ESV)*

Use the power of these words daily to break down the stronghold of a victim spirit that has tainted your life and delayed the blessing of your destiny.

THE PRESENCE OF THE FRUIT OF THE SPIRIT

"Paul has been preaching about the call of God to freedom, and so he now spells it out: we are done with the demands of the law; now we are free to live in the Spirit and to be truly right with God. As free people, the Spirit gives us the characteristics of Jesus; we, too, can freely love in joy and peace. We can have patience along with kindness and faithfulness that can only come from the Father. We can reflect the goodness of God while being gentle in operating with self-control. For those who follow Him and live in the Spirit, these characteristics or fruits are a gift from God. As we grow in the faith, we find that we belong to God and can walk daily in the Spirit." (Galatians 5:22, VOICE)

> *"But the fruit of the Spirit is love, joy, peace, forbearance, kindness, goodness, faithfulness, gentleness and self-control. Against such things there is no law."*
> — *(Galatians 5:22, 23, NIV)*

41

> "The Father is sending a great Helper, the Holy Spirit, in My name to teach you everything and to remind you of all I have said to you."
> — *(John 14:26, VOICE)*

> "(for the fruit of the light consists in all goodness, righteousness and truth)."
> — *(Ephesians 5:9, NIV)*

> "May the God of hope fill you with all joy and peace as you trust in him, so that you may overflow with hope by the power of the Holy Spirit."
> — *(Romans 15:13, NIV)*

> "But you, man of God (woman), flee from all this, and pursue righteousness, godliness, faith, love, endurance and gentleness".
> — *(1 Timothy 6:11, NIV/Italics added)*

THE DISCIPLINES OF A SOUND MIND

> "We are coming to the end of all things, so be serious and keep your wits about you in order to pray more forcefully."
> — *1 Peter 4:7, VOICE)*

> No discipline seems pleasant at the time, but painful. Later on, however, it produces a harvest of righteousness and peace for those who have been trained by it.
> — **Hebrews 12:11, NIV**

Because you have been working through the strengthening areas illustrated above, "The Power of God's Word," "The Presence of the Fruit of the Spirit," and "The Disciplines of a Sound Mind," your struggles are coming to an end of their hold and control over your life. You are no longer a victim of your circumstances and you are becoming all that God has called and anointed you to be. Your potential and the ability to live your life without limits is tied to the wealth of your thoughts. If your thinking is bankrupt, then what's produced in your life will be empty and worthless. When we approach our thoughts as learned skills and abilities, we understand that we can learn new skills and practice them to improve our lives, our relationships and more importantly, our decisions. When we take the time to discipline our minds, we will not be guilty of going around the same issue year in and year out. There is nothing more important than a disciplined mind, no matter where you may be in life, or whatever your situation or circumstance may be. You may be experiencing the lowest moment in your life. But you, too, can come out of this and overcome it by bringing your mind into alignment with sound thoughts. Stinking, defeated, victimized thinking will eventually cause problems, and wasted time and energy, which ultimately leads to frustration, emotional downfalls, and pain. Having a disciplined mind means stretching your thoughts to use the positive information you have uploaded through the three disciplines we discussed earlier. Every discussion and life decision must be measured by the Word. You have taken 21 days to read, study and memorize God's Word. If applied daily, it is the only guarantee to heal broken emotions and broken lives, as well as change your life. All of us have a multitude of choices to make on any given day. For us to make sound choices, we must draw on the information we have placed in our minds. If the information we have received all our life has been corrupt, vile, self-defeating, paranoid, or simply wrong, the choices we make will reflect that information. When we use the ingested Word of God, it pushes us to ask questions to make sure that the direction we're going is God's way. We may ask questions like: Am I seeing things right? What's really going on? Are they being honest or trying to take advantage of me? Does this person or people really care about me, or is this just a casual situation? Will this decision benefit me and others? Will I become better, richer, stronger, or greater by going in this direction? Responding well to these and other questions will be the litmus test of the Word we have placed inside our minds. The Bible teaches us to guard our heart, and it interchanges *heart* with *mind*. (Proverbs 4:23) If we can apply the *mind* to this passage, we find guard your *mind* for out of it flow the issues of life! This Scripture I've loosely quoted warns us that our minds need to be guarded. A better way of understanding this is to say *critiqued*, tested to find the quality of our thinking. Our thoughts and ultimately our actions must be measured by the abundance of God's Word and His love. When we take every thought captive and every idea that exalts itself above our knowledge of God, we are disciplining our minds to be sound. Don't allow wild random thoughts to cloud your mind. It would also be good to find someone positive, someone you respect to run your thoughts past, someone who knows you and your old thought patterns to help you stay on track and to help you bring every thought into alignment with your new and renewed thoughts. Remember, the development of a sound mind takes time and you must commit to it for the long term.

My Mind and Life Reloaded

> *"Do not allow this world to mold you in its own image. Instead, be transformed from the inside out by renewing your mind. As a result, you will be able to discern what God wills and whatever God finds good, pleasing, and complete."*
> — *(Romans 12:2, VOICE)*

Whenever anyone moves to change their life, it must always begin with a change of mind. If you can get your mind out of bondage, your body will follow! Over the past few chapters, you have begun the hard work of getting rid of old thoughts, stagnant beliefs, stinking thinking, and living your life in fear. It is now time to rebuild your empty soul, because if we leave it cleaned out and empty, the things you got rid of will soon return. Rebuilding your soul must begin with courage. You will need the courage to choose the things you have never chosen before, and the first choice is love. The foundation of your life must begin with love. I know it will take courage to open your heart to give and receive the greatest gift of all, which is love. We must first invite the gift of love from our Creator into our lives. When it comes into our hearts, it also permeates our minds so that our words and actions are laced with the love of God. The pattern of this great love is that our outward expression cannot be greater than our inward quality. Scripture teaches that our outward expression of words and actions amount to nothing if the inward quality of love is empty. By beginning to upload our clean minds and hearts with some of the promises of love from God, it will, over time, set the foundation of who you are, as well as increase the depth of what's inside.

45

These promises are found in 1 Corinthians 13:

Love Never Gives Up.

Love Cares More for Others than for Self.

Love Doesn't Want What It Doesn't Have.

Love Doesn't Strut.

Love Doesn't Have a Swelled Head.

Love Doesn't Keep Score of the Sins of Others.

Love Doesn't Revel When Others Grovel.

Love Takes Pleasure in the Flowering of Truth.

Love Puts Up With Anything.

Love Trusts God Always.

Love Always Looks for the Best.

Love Never Looks Back but Keeps Going to the End.

Love Never Dies.

We have three things to do to lead us toward that consummation: Trust steadily in God; hope unswervingly; love extravagantly. And the best of the three is love! *(Taken from The Message).*

Learning to love yourself is the hardest change you will encounter, especially if you never learned your value or that you matter. It's clear that loving yourself or bonding with yourself brings balance, self-healing, and provides relational strength. Let's begin by binding with the principles of love. The first one is, "*Love never gives up.*" So as you come face to face with pain, hurt and maybe frustration, don't back up into your old self, but take responsibility for your feelings while covering them in this new-found love. Make sure that this time you don't abandon your need to matter, but you qualify your feelings based on the knowledge of your importance, uniqueness and original design by God. The second one is, "<u>Love cares more for others than for self.</u>" This step will be tricky because of the tendency to discount yourself. This principle is not telling you to think nothing of yourself; it is saying that when you are involved with another person, real love will seek to serve that person first, and then yourself. It is never instructing you to neglect the complete person you're learning to become. You assist others out of the abundance of love you carry for yourself which can be easily neglected until it becomes part of your everyday life. Stepping into this type of learning helps your personal love life grow, so that you don't fall into old behavior of denying responsibility for your feelings, and then backing into addictive or controlling behavior. In this instance, lean on God's unconditional love knowing that there is nothing you can do to change His feelings for you. The third one is, "*Love Doesn't Want What It Doesn't Have.*" We are all guilty of comparing ourselves to others or feeling we should have what they have. This emotion is called Envy and it is the darkness of Jealousy. Nothing can ruin a sunny day like wanting what you don't have. Don't get this emotion twisted; it is not ambition when we see someone with equal or identical desires and we are moved to push until we have attained what is desired. True ambition competes with itself and does not envy the success or achievements of others.

Ambitious people can celebrate the accomplishments of others knowing they are next in line. However, envy and jealousy not only want your place in line, they seek to push you out of line altogether. The upload of a God-given love does not walk this road or participate with those who do. One of the best ways to get rid of envy and jealousy is to never forget the milestones in your life. Celebrate your victories and don't forget them; they will encourage you to push forward. To be able to do that, you have to determine your call and purpose. What God has placed in your heart that you desire to fulfil, put your finger on that! Then with every inch of your strength, fight for it. Be thankful for how far you've come with every step of the way. Remember, *jealousy* means wanting what you don't have. The end of it will kill your joy as you pursue your purpose.

The fourth and fifth ones are, *"Love Doesn't Strut"* and *"Love Doesn't Have a Swelled Head."* The love transplant you received will never engage in the sin of self-glory or vainglory. As you become successful with your transformation and you see successes happening often in your life, you will need to keep guard of issues that come to hinder your growth. Strutting your stuff with a swelled head is a big one! This enemy known as *pride*, self-glory or vainglory will bite you and destroy everything you have accomplished to this point. According to St. Thomas Aquinas, there is nothing wrong with others recognizing our good qualities and deeds. In fact, seeking to live in a way that inspires others to give glory to God and to pursue a more virtuous life is good. However, seeking human praise, applause, and glory for *its own sake* is sinful, detrimental, and harmful to your forward move toward your God-designed destiny. We must be careful that we are not drawn to the wrong people, seeking their approval when their integrity is in question. All glory belongs to God, and honour for you will follow your good deeds. Vainglory, when we seek its fruit, will bring seeds of other issues like hypocrisy. The Greek meaning for *hypocrite* is actor or pretender. What it's saying is that this type of person is acting or pretending and seeking approval based on something that's not real. When you seek public approval, just like milk left out on a hot day, we spoil the gift we're trying to present to God.

"Love Doesn't Keep Score of the Sins of Others," "Love Doesn't Revel When Others Grovel," but *"Love Takes Pleasure in the Flowering of Truth."* The Holy Spirit, through the direction and design of God, has uploaded certain attributes that can be seen and recognized by others. The first is your willingness to forgive the mistakes, missteps and hurts imposed on you by others. It is such a rich infusion of God's love that you choose to forget the sins others have committed against you. Your character becomes so sound and stable that you are not happy when others are hurting and that you always seek truth in all that you do. These outward signs of an inward change are an unspoken testimony to all who are watching your life, and for those who are waiting for you to fail. This infusion of the God-kind of love must become the foundation of who you are and how you respond to everything without respect of person or circumstance.

Once you have established a pattern of running your life according to God's design and exhibiting characteristics of His "Love Language," it will be time to move to the next mind and life reload.

LIVING IN DESTINY NOW

Destiny living is possibility living or better yet, it is impossibility living! If you have taken in everything offered from the previous chapters, you have worked yourself from a place of not believing you matter. Go to a mirror, now look deeply into your own eyes; you can literately see you have grown to this impossible place. This is the place of knowing you are not just a conqueror, you're "more than a conqueror!" You were someone that others have discounted as being less than, not really mattering. But today, you are right here in the reality of your personal growth and beginning your walk of destiny. There are certain things you have to learn as you walk out the destiny that's ordered by the Lord. These principles are called "Destiny Knowledge (DK)," so let's get started. DK Principle One: *"Your attitude is in your hands."* DK living supports your understanding that how you approach living is your choice. Life is hard and there will always be hardships, but how you face them is up to you. Say to yourself: *I no longer give my power to other people or life's trials.* Choose to live with the power that you cannot always control what comes into your life, but you can control how you respond. Your attitude frames how you think about what's happening to you. You have been given the power of the Holy Spirit and the responsibility from God to control what you can, and that is your attitude.

Two men were confined to hospital room beds; they were roommates. One complained loudly of having only a white wall to stare at every day, while his roommate had the window. So, his roommate offered to tell him what he saw. The roommate described beautiful sunlit days with an array of flowers bursting forth with every color of the rainbow. There were children running and playing on rolling fields of green and tall grass. He told the roommate of beautiful butterflies, hummingbirds, and beautiful sparrows singing in the distance. He told of families enjoying a meal and lovers holding each other in the grass. The roommate's daily graphic description would soon put the other man in such a calm attitude he would fall asleep as he envisioned the heavenly view. Soon the roommate with the window was gone, and the man learned he died of his aliment. The man requested to be moved to the window so he could see for himself what was described by his roommate. When the man was moved to the window, he quickly threw open the blinds only to find a disfigured brick wall outside the window. He wondered why his roommate did not complain as he had. He concluded that his roommate chose to see heaven while he chose to see a blank white wall. Our DK lesson has to do with attitude; it is your choice! Developing and living with the right attitude is not a new thing. The Bible speaks about our disposition and attitude when the Apostle Paul told us to not be anxious about anything, but with prayer and personal pleas, make your request to God Who has the power to change everything. The Scripture goes on to tell you what to think in order to have the right attitude to fuel your destiny travel. It says, *"Summing it all up, friends, I'd say you'll do best by filling your minds and meditating on things true, noble, reputable, authentic, compelling, gracious—the best, not the worst; the beautiful, not the ugly; things to praise, not things to curse. Put into practice what you learned from me, what you heard and saw and realized. Do that, and God, who makes everything work together, will work you into his most excellent* harmonies." (Philippians 4:8, 9, MSG)

The art of replacement comes with knowing and understanding the thoughts that have kept you bound. When the thoughts of bondage come to overwhelm your mind and paralyze your movement, this is the time practicing the art of filling that space with things that are true and beautiful proves to usher you into your next level of living.

DESTINY KNOWLEDGE

> *"Each of us, as a good manager of God's different gifts, must use for the good of others the special gift we have received from God."*
> *— (1 Peter 4:10, Good News Translation, GNT)*

Knowing who and what God called them for is everyone's pursuit and their desire for destiny. Most of us hold our happiness within the fingertips of the time it takes us to learn and work in the place God has appointed just for us. Living, moving and being all that He has ordained for us is the world's ultimate desire. Your need for gaining Destiny Knowledge must be intentional. You are working that knowledge with God, allowing Him to pull you in the direction He wants you to go. It's imperative for you to move in that direction so that you don't find yourself going back into what God has rescued you from, having and living by your knowledge and understanding that God has created you on purpose for a purpose.

You are not an accident or something unwanted; God intended for you to be here at this time, in this place and for His specific reason. Until you come to know that place, you must approach life knowing God has a purpose for you. With your intentional creation, God brought you into this world with specific gifts that He intends for you to use to help others, and for you to prosper. At this point, the most important thing for you to do is discover the gifts God has placed in your life. These gifts show up as assets, things you seem to be naturally good at doing. Your personality, your looks, your intelligence etc. These gifts are based on what God has placed in your life spiritually, as well as what you seem to love or have a heart for doing. It could be acts that are no sweat for you to do. We have all been given the responsibility by God to work through our gifts for the good of others and for the glory of God. We are to work it to the best of our ability and not get caught up in comparisons of our God-given abilities. These are spiritual gifts because our God is a spirit. But the gifts or abilities play out in our lives so that we live lives full of the power of God or the Holy Spirit. These gifts are given to bless and benefit others while simultaneously blessing and benefiting the person using the gift. Every child of God has at least one gift and your responsibility is to find out what that gift is and how God would like that gift expressed. God, our Father runs a successful business and His product is people. Every child born into His family are brought into His business. Each give special and specific gifts to benefit the entire family and the people you are sent to touch. God doesn't have picks and chooses where some kids are given more than others because He just likes them better. No, He encourages all His children to "(Seek) … earnestly the best gifts. But now let me show you a way of life that is best of all, always remembering for what they are given." Scripture goes on to say that these gifts must be exercised in and by the love of God. So, having these gifts is your birthright, but coming to grips with using them can be intimidating, even strange at times. Working through the knowledge of the gift and how God wants to use them is your greatest feat, keeping in mind that your gifts can be manipulated by others and abused by you. Misuse of your gifts has the potential to be dangerous and detrimental to you. Think about how many have received unnecessary church when a gift has gone rogue. When used wrongly, the same gift that provided comfort and assistance to many can be explosively destructive. This may be one reason some are tempted not to use their gifts at all. This can only happen when you stop seeking God on the daily use of your gifts. It is so important when you put your gifts to work that whatever you do, it brings glory and honor to our Father, God. Pursuing love and desiring spiritual gifts are not disconnected. These gifts are given to God's children to help us love each other. You must know that you are a unique member of Christ's Body, and each of us has a unique function and unique gifts to benefit the world and the family of God for our common good. Our gifts are not for us to become important seeking our moment in the spotlight. These gifts are for the greater good of people and the greater glory of Christ. Knowing your gift gives your life purpose, direction, and power. It's hard to sit feeling sorry for ourselves when we are loving and seeking the greater good for others. Love is the aim of your gift. It is possible to possess and exercise these gifts without love, but the Bible tells us that if we work this way, we are nothing. The other side of that is if we remain intimated by these gifts, we in essence neglect the benefit God has given us, and we remain in an unfulfilled life, living out the dreaded life of a victim of circumstances, instead of being a victor of our stance. The Bible is not a how-to manual; it is a treasure chest of golden nuggets that we must seek, dig, and pursue to find them. You having the desire to do it is the test, but this same desire fuels your quest to know and do. This is the simple truth in your quest of understanding and living out the blessings in the Bible. Seeking this out is just like when you want something badly; you don't just wait around for someone to decide to put a ribbon on it and bring it to you, do you? No; you go looking, seeking, asking questions of people able to give you directions about what you want. For things not readily visible, you may read appropriate material, watch, and listen to a lot of information to gain what you're looking for. The Bible teaches us to ask, seek, and knock (Matthew 7:7), if you really want what you're seeking. The value of the object sought is worth all the hard work you put into having it. Begin utilizing this fantastic gift by soaking up the Word of God concerning spiritual gifts; pray about how He would like you to use your unique gifts. Finally, do not fail to come into the company of like-minded children of God, being open to hear their teachings and testimonies. These steps will give you fuel for your journey and increased knowledge for your quest to be used of God.

Your ability to flow in the gifts of God is entirely up to you. God gives them freely; there are no rejects. But I also believe the biggest reason the Body of Christ hasn't made a significant impact on this generation today is because of our failure to seek to operate in the gifts given to us. It is very clear that Jesus and the early disciples used their gifts like a magnet, attracting large crowds to them to hear the good news, and confirming that God was the orchestrator of their gifts. When we feel the love of God flowing through us toward someone, and we reach out to show His love to that person, we are flowing in the gift God has given which is always fueled by His overshadowing love for mankind. Often, you feel drawn to people, and knowing them is a prerequisite to flowing in the love of God through your gifts. You are to embrace the unction and move in the direction God is directing you to. It may be just to give that person a word that God loves them. From there, God may fill your mind with the right things at the right moment to minister to the needs of those around you. It is important that you know you matter deeply to God, so you don't allow your insecurities to overcome moving in the direction God is pulling you.

As I conclude my discussion on the gifts of the Spirit, I would like to share that I received a note from an exceptional young woman. This young woman has been groomed all her life to do great exploits for the Lord. She has pursued many things in her life, even earning a doctorate degree. She is a woman with three beautiful children. She recently sent her oldest off to college as an avid athlete. She has worked many places and has owned a business for children and at this time, she is counseling and lending her expertise wherever there is a need. Her resumé is impressive, and, on the surface, she appears to have it all together. But her email reveals something deeper going on inside her heart and spirit. She enjoys people and doing things in, around and for the church, as well as her family and community. Her husband heard the call of the Lord and together they started a ministry, which became a small community church. But her note sounded distressed, almost depressed. Finally, she began by sharing her memories of her childhood. She wrote,

"There is a song that was sung in the church when I was a child. I used to sing it and enjoy declaring my decision to follow Christ. 'I have decided to follow Jesus ... No turning back, no turning back.'" I too had a memory of this song. The melody would flow from our seats to the ceiling and seemed to catch the wings of the wind as the harmony of the crowd elevated to full vibrato. The words and the willingness of the congregants and leaders alike singing at the top of their lungs gave me the feeling of warmth and acceptance.

"Lately," she wrote, "it seems like the song and lyrics cross my mind daily." I thought it was as if her soul was seeking what her mind can't capture. She went on to write, "But I can't sing it anymore! Not right now. It's too touching. Not the part about following Jesus; I have no problem with that; it is what I do daily." I thought yes, following Jesus is our daily bread, our breath, and our reason for living. "It's the verse that says, 'Tho' none go with me, I still will follow.' Really God? If I looked back and no one was standing there, would I be alright with it?" Her question made me shudder. The naked reality of the possibility of no one being there to back us, uphold us and to cover us is a harsh reality to view. "Honestly," she went on to write, "I think my answer is 'no.'"

This brilliant, anointed young woman continued, "I'm not singing this song for now as I search my heart and soul to determine why it is so difficult for me to say 'yes' again. Why do I entertain the voice or perception of the crowd? Is the crowd there or is the crowd really me? Why, after all this time, am I still tripping over the fact that some days I'll be left standing with little support, little encouragement, and only God on my side? Perhaps, it's because I, too, just want to matter to people and to God!"

What hurts more than pangs of regret? It's one of the worst feelings in the world, right? Once we move from the nagging pain and the rehearsing of failed opportunities, we can then move to a place where we learn from our letdown. Regret comes in many forms. I put God first on that list of things we hate—that we have let Him down. Then we move to education, career, romance, and parenting just to name a few from research I reviewed. Regret is followed by feelings of   dissatisfaction and disappointment. These feelings are stronger when the opportunity for corrective action wasn't taken. I believe our greatest regret is missed opportunity. Procrastination is a close second, causing regret over things we just don't do. While living through the effects of regret, we must be careful not to allow its negative influence to cause us to lose confidence and withdraw, not wanting to be around people. Regret will also cause us to beat ourselves up more than is necessary. Overcoming regret begins with taking corrective measures to change the behavior that caused the issues in the first place. Overcoming regret should move us to goals we either didn't set or didn't follow in the beginning. Failing to do the background work for the things we tried to accomplish, assist us in failing and dealing with the consequences of regret. None of us are perfect so we are either feeling it right now, or we're on the road to suffering the effects of failure.

The question that those who are suffering the effects of regret are asking is, 'How do you get out of regret?' Understand that when you are experiencing regret, you are evaluating a bad situation that happened in the past with the awareness, insight and understanding you have in the present.

This is how it plays out: You make plans, but something happens. You react; you make a choice, and you act. Then time passes. Finally, you think about what happened. You analyze it, often obsess over it, and talk about it every time and any time someone will listen. Usually your friends go through the suffering with you. Since you do want to grow, you continue to gather more information and knowledge. Then, taking all this awareness and information that you have now, you beat yourself up because you did not know it back *then*. It is not right and reasonable for you to take what you know now and use it to beat yourself up for what you didn't know then.

The blessing about regret is that it gets your attention and opens the door for you to walk into God's opportunity for learning and transformation. But in order to do that, you must stop driving while looking in the rearview mirror, and you must let go of the shoulda/coulda/wouldas!

> *"Of all sad words of tongue or pen,*
> *the saddest are these, 'It might have been!'"*
> — *John Greenleaf Whittier*

The best and most effective way to deal with regret is to seek the assistance of God. God assists us into moving our negative feelings of regret into a positive position that motivates us to action.

Prior to his conversion, Paul had been a determined persecutor of the Christian Way. He was a missionary of mayhem who sought to destroy the church of God. But those bloody days were not without lingering regrets, even after his soul had been redeemed and cleansed by Jesus Christ. The apostle did not wither away, indulging himself in self-pity and unproductive anxiety. Rather, he channeled his memories into a fiery zeal that would take him into three missionary campaigns and other preaching adventures on behalf of the gospel of Christ. He resolutely endured persecution and was made stronger for it. If you have done everything biblically possible to take care of past mistakes in the face of your regrets by calling those things that are not as though they are true, and by refusing to allow regret to control and disable you. Take a stance that you will use every painful moment of it to push you to a higher good for God. It will be more than you might have accomplished without the letdowns, failures, or pushbacks. To come away from the debilitating effects of regret takes effort and the right attitude. The Bible teaches that we are to renew our minds (Romans 12:2). So how do we do this in a practical daily way? We begin working on the inside first. There are attitudes we need to put on each day to live out our God-given destiny. Let's begin these recovery steps, going back to Romans 8:6 which tells us our minds need to be in the right spirit to move forward in life. It tells us to be "spiritually minded," which means to have a peaceful mind and an attitude full of love and joy. This is a choice; the alternative is that we choose to have a negative attitude lacking peace, love, and joy. What you are doing by commanding your mind to have certain attitudes is establishing a predisposition for healthy, wholesome and a God-like, disposition. This predisposition is worked out in your daily life by you presenting yourself available and willing to give God permission to work within you as only He can. When you struggle with regret, it is difficult to imagine what life would be like if you came to grips with the issue and found the strength to move forward with your life. To begin with, you must name what's bringing you down. What is the root of your regret? Is it shame, hurt, or abandonment? If you are struggling with more than one feeling, name them; make a list if need be. Begin with pulling down these towers that want to hide you in the shadows of regret. Listen to what your feelings are saying. For example: I really messed that up; I should have done it like I planned it! What a stupid mistake! I will never be asked again! You then begin to tell yourself the truth. The truth is what sets our spirits free. All really isn't lost; it really isn't the end of the world, or the end of your world! Most likely, you will be asked, invited, or scheduled again! After going through each one and telling yourself the truth about the issue, it's time to "Let it go!" Burn it. Bury it. Tear it up. Forget it and dare it to return! If this issue tries to slither back into your mind, tell it loud and clear to, STOP! More importantly, forgive yourself the mistakes you've made and forgive anyone you're blaming for your hurt, pain or issues. If you can ask them to forgive your attitude or actions as a result of the issue, this single act frees your heart, mind and spirit. It also provides the peace that only God can give. The Bible teaches us that God demands that we clear these relationship issues prior to speaking with Him or offering Him anything. The bottom line is that you take action to move forward instead of being paralyzed to just sit there being angry, hurt or dismayed, which is an unhealthy toxic situation. Then begin to walk in newness of life, as if everything has rolled off your shoulders like water off a duck's back. Start claiming your freedom until your heart and feelings agree with your declaration. When you're overcome with negativity, push back and declare over and over again until what you say becomes what you know! (Lisa Kyle n.d.)

In a nutshell, I am suggesting steps to help you overcome and get past regret in your life and they are:

1. Make peace with yourself.
2. Turn adversity into opportunity.
3. Stop playing the role of 'victim.'
4. Make every day count.

When we begin to live by the above principles, we gain the peace that God gives. *"I am leaving you with a gift – peace of mind and heart! And the peace I give isn't fragile like the peace the world gives. So, don't be troubled or afraid."* (John 14:27, The Living Bible, *TLB*) The Bible teaches that God has a peace that's not weak or soft like a marshmallow, but is the strength that comes from God Himself. This peace can take it and still stand up in you for whatever comes after. Walking in our path to purpose is to find our passion. It is important that you spend time examining yourself to find out what you have a passion for. It may be one thing or ten things; these things need to cover your ideal life without limitations of time, place, and money. Take time to write down what your ideal passion is and what you would do if you didn't have to worry about the 'how.' How to get there? How to put it together? How to get help? How to pay for it? You just need to deal right now with the "What." Grab a piece of paper and number it 1-15 and begin dreaming. Dream God-size dreams, out-of-this-world dreams, things that would bring you absolute happiness, joy, and love. Dream no-boundary dreams, no-strings-attached dreams. Allow God to free your mind and spirit to fill you with the plans He has for you, to bring you to an expected end. When you search inside to find your passion, what you're asking yourself is, What's driving your life? Is it fear? Is it anger? Is it regret? Is it ambition? Is it hope, but no work? Or have you been pushed by the desire to please others? Or is it something as frivolous as the accumulation of possessions? Finding your passion is opening the door to your purpose. Many pastors and teachers have identified important life-changing points, that God intends to be a driving force in your life's quest of living with passion and working on purpose. Several pastors have compiled their own lists and from their teaching and statements, their collective list implies the following:

1. God planned for us to know Him and love Him, which brings Him pleasure.
2. We were wired with a need to find a home, family, and mainly to be part of God's family.
3. God created us to become like Christ, full of His love, joy, peace, patience, kindness, goodness, faithfulness, gentleness, and self-control.
4. We were designed to serve God with our unique mix of talents, skills, and passions.
5. Our created life plan is to introduce other people to God and His purposes for their lives, too.

When you are unsure of God's desire and plan for you, you become driven by destructive influences, because we are all motivated by something, positive or negative. Everyone is driven toward divine purpose or designated destruction. It is your job to choose which way you want to go. Knowing your purpose gives meaning to your life. The only way to know it is first to know God and then to understand why you are here. Without your Godly purpose, life has no meaning and ultimately, no significance. Death is not the greatest tragedy. Living a life without purpose is greater!

CHAPTER FOUR

NEXT-LEVEL LIVING

Expect God's promotion. "For exaltation comes
neither from the east nor from the west nor from
the south. But God is the Judge: He puts down one,
and exalts another." Psalm 75:6, 7, NKJV);
"Therefore humble yourselves under the mighty
hand of God, that He may exalt you (raise you up)
in due time.
(1 Peter 5:6, NKJV)

In the previous chapters, you have been confronting the issues that
caused you to question your value and to repeatedly ask yourself,
"Do I Matter?" If you have followed the suggestions and worked it
until it works for you, you are now in a place to move to your next
level of elevation. I am not talking about arrival at a destination but
moving within the journey God has designed specifically for you,
because this is your elevation. When you lived in a place of not
knowing your passion and purpose, it was like living underground,

undercover, not being exposed to His magnificent light. When you start stepping out of that old life, it is like stepping into your elevation elevator. You may have pushed the top floor, but the elevation is one floor at a time. Our celebration is that you are moving away from the basement. Although Scripture indicates your steps are ordered by the Lord, this implies your direction is predetermined by God if you are following His guidance. (Psalm 37:33) It is Gods desire and pleasure that you walk in the newness of life He has provided for you. This next-level living is what He has in mind for you. You were not created to live beneath His design, but He is a gentleman and will not force you to accept what He has graciously prepared for you. It is the enemy of our faith that constantly bombards our mind and emotions with our limitations, trying to constrain you from the possibility that you are better than you think and greater than you realize. God has placed an overflow of greatness inside of you. It is up to you to say yes to the greatness in you. When you give yourself permission to be great, the power and strength inside you has been lying dormant, waiting for the day and opportunity to be pulled out. I am inviting you to know there is power in your Yes!

There is still fear, though, because all these years you have believed the lie that you would always be underground, always stuck, never having enough strength to change your life. But you must move even if you are afraid; you must move, shaking, unsure, unsupported, or unknown. It is your destiny! When you embrace God's truth about you, it clears your sight for everything as you move forward. Before you got to the power of your yes, your vision was obstructed or blurred.

It's like going to the eye doctor and they decide to dilate your pupils. This procedure gives the eye doctor the ability to see any abnormalities in your eyes, but it also distorts what you see for a while until the effects wear off. Buildings, people, cars and chairs seem larger than they really are. They seem to move when they are stationary. The treatment makes you nervous about doing what you know you can do! It's like doing simple things like driving, because life is distorted due to what's going on with you. This description is similar to what happens when the enemy has distorted your view where he makes you believe things are worse than they really are. It seems problems are bigger than they really are, which in turn causes you to feel like you can't do what you know you're capable of doing. Just as I stated before, this is not a destination; it is a journey. You are seeking generally what you should be moving toward for the rest of your life. I believe that God gives each of us a generalized purpose that is worked out through assignments placed in our lives. Damion indicated how much he loved helping people, but he wasn't sure what his passion was. We discussed what he was doing now to help others. He stated that he is open to their needs and supportive of their problems and issues. Damion said others seek him as a kind but strong listener who gives good advice. I asked how he felt about this role. He described how he always finds himself in this position, even from when he was very young, and he feels valued and needed when he is in this role. Damion never tires of being available for people in this way and he always seems to know just what to say. Because he was searching for his own purpose, which prompted our conversation. Bringing yourself to this type of self-examination will always point to your purpose in life, if it is helping others and fulfilling a need in your life, too.

Don't Camp Out in Your Comfort Zone

The book of Deuteronomy was written by Moses, a book to remind Israel of Who loves them; what really matters; what is right and what is wrong. It's a transitional book. When we are wandering around trying to find our purpose and direction, we are in a transitional period. Just like Israel, God will never leave us hopeless and wandering. He will bring you to an expected end and help you along the way. Well, for forty years, the nation of Israel was just wandering, not knowing their purpose, having lost their focus and direction. The root of Deuteronomy is *Deutero*, which means *second*, and *nomos*, which means *law*. Deuteronomy is the second hearing of the law, or a chance to rediscover what God has spoken over your life to take you to the next-level living. I truly understand why many may not want to go to the next level, if we read Deuteronomy 1:6-8 in *The Message* Bible.

> "Back at Horeb, GOD, our God, spoke to us: 'You've stayed long enough at this mountain. On your way now. Get moving. Head for the Amorite hills, wherever people are living in the Arabah, the mountains, the foothills, the Negev, the seashore—the Canaanite country and the Lebanon all the way to the big river, the Euphrates. Look, I've given you this land. Now go in and take it. It's the land GOD promised to give your ancestors Abraham, Isaac, and Jacob and their children after them.'"

We find the place God was leading His people to was full of unexpected enemies. They needed to prepare for people who are not happy about their elevation or promotion. You will have to be ready to take friendly fire, which is extremely painful. It's like David said, in my words, "I could have taken it if it wasn't you!" My friend, my fellow laborer, or my brother and sister in the Lord will either attack you or worse, ignore you as being less than significant. But you must understand that God wants you to fulfil your purpose and to answer His call, because you are written in His vision on Earth, and there is a part you must play.

Overcoming Wilderness Mentality

God has not called us to fail! But the ability to view failure as a setup to next-level living is the difference between average people who give up and exceptional people who press on. Life is full of promise if we live, try, push, fail and get up and try all over again. There is a huge gap between average people or those who have settled for the comfort of mediocrity, and those who setup to exceptional living. That difference is how they respond to the changes occurring daily in their lives. When you exercise the ability of stepping outside the failure, knowing it's not you that failed, it's the attempt you made that failed. By accepting this knowledge and stepping outside your fear of failure, you are changing your mental definition of failure. So, instead of you taking it personally and nursing your pain, you act and use that energy to push you forward. Stand firm and determine not to allow outside influences that bring negativity and fear to stand firm inside. Close your mental door on all of yesterday's negativity. Changing your mindset empowers you to change your atmosphere and change your world. At the end of every bad moment or event, take it apart and see what you can learn and benefit from through the experience. By doing this, you will be able to work on your weaknesses causing them to become your new strength, so that when success does come your way and it will, it should push you to try something harder. There is truly not much difference between a person of success and one of failure expect one worked past the obstacles and the other gave up. Remember, success is a path you intentionally seek, find, and follow. This also includes taking only those with the same view in mind on this path with you. Otherwise, people along for the ride change the dynamics of your success journey and don't add value to it. There is a song that says, "One day at a time, sweet Jesus," and our journey to live out our God-given success is one day at a time. Begin and end each day acknowledging its accomplishments and you will be a step closer to seeing the totality of what you were created to be. I know that some days you would rather stay in bed and forget about being a success. You lay there in anticipation of some surge of motivation flooding through your body and mind that never comes, and because it doesn't come, you don't move! And another day bites the dust and you haven't progressed toward your goals. I want to encourage you to get going even if you are not motivated, even if your motivation never comes or floods your body and mind. Take Nike's motto "Just Do It." Get up and just do what you have planned to do! Do it completely and intentionally no matter how you feel. From this day forward you will cease to work and move by your feelings; you will work and move intentionally going forward. Right at this moment of growth, I declare and decree in your life not just success but the success of God which is Great Success as you move from wilderness mentality to Kingdom mentality!

My Mind Unchained

> *"But that's no life for you. You learned Christ! My assumption is that you have paid careful attention to him, been well instructed in the truth precisely as we have it in Jesus. Since, then, we do not have the excuse of ignorance, everything—and I do mean everything—connected with that old way of life has to go. It's rotten through and through. Get rid of it! And then take on an entirely new way of life—a God-fashioned life, a life renewed from the inside and working itself into your conduct as God accurately reproduces his character in you."*
> *— (Ephesians 4: 20-24, MSG)*

In life, when we struggle with knowing if we matter in the world, we must first begin the work in our mind. The mind is powerful and if we don't purposely think about our thoughts we can be led astray in the wrong direction. Our thoughts about how we feel about ourselves are formed when we are young by those significant people in our lives such as parents, and as we grow and develop relationships outside of our parents, the thoughts about ourselves get shaped by friends, teachers, and media influence. If we go through life accepting and buying into all the outside influences, we are guaranteed to lose ourselves.

It's no secret that our worth begins to diminish based upon negative feedback and if left unchecked, it can take us on a downward slope. Each negative experience represents a chain placed on our mind. So, for every disappointment, every rejection, every time we were told we weren't good enough or smart enough, we have a chain that captured our mind and beliefs in those areas.

Chains are designed for multiple purposes. Some are used for mere decoration; some are used for power transfer; some are used for security and restraint; some are used for traction and pulling, and some are used for weapons. They are all pretty much made of links of metal that are attached to one another. The type of metal depends on their purpose. The chains of negative words have linked themselves together to the point that we can't accurately receive positive words to help us and validate who we truly are so that we can see that we do matter in this life. The chains in our mind serve two purposes. The first is security and restraint. The second is a weapon. Let's examine these two types of chains that exist in our minds.

The chains that serve the purpose of safety and restraint probably sound like an oxymoron type of thought. I mean, if we are holding on to negative things that challenge our self-worth and value, how can it possibly be a safety and restraint mechanism? Well, I'm glad you asked. The reason it's a safety and restraint mechanism is because after years of thinking and focusing on negative thoughts, they actually begin to become all we know; we begin to find comfort and solace in them. Those thoughts and feelings of rejection and not feeling good enough become a part of life for us to the point that we can no longer see the reality of those not being true. The chains work to keep any positive words from those that recognize our worth. The chains prevent God's Word from coming in to renew our mind as He instructs us. The chains also protect us from the hurt of rejection, but because it is an oxymoron to begin with, the chains that we think protect us from people hurting us are actually causing more hurt, because people can't love us and we can't receive God's love. They leave us empty of anything positive and they cause loneliness, depression, and bitterness. Ultimately, they cause us to feel as though we don't matter.

So, how do we unchain our minds from these thoughts and feelings?

We must begin to purposely change our thoughts. Our thoughts are powerful, but we do have the power to change them. Sometimes it may require therapy; sometimes it may require medication, and ultimately it requires prayer asking God to help us. But it is possible to change our thoughts, which will change our hearts, what we feel, and ultimately help us to know that we absolutely matter to God and to others.

I know a woman who was raised in a home with her parents, but they never provided her with any emotional or spiritual support. They had a very toxic relationship which made for a toxic environment. This woman had an aunt who provided her with the emotional support she needed, but in all that, she did to try to make up for what her parents did not have the capacity to do; however, it didn't feel the void. The woman shared that she spent countless hours alone in her room listening to violence take place in her home. She was exposed to drug use and all types of negative things. Her parents never told her she was loved or hugged her. So, she went through life believing she didn't matter to anyone. The enemy was able to reinforce those thought patterns over and over in her life. She felt so worthless that she attempted to take her life at age 12! She made multiple attempts throughout her teenage years and even into her early 20s.

This woman was well into her 30s before she truly realized that if she didn't begin to change her thoughts, she was going to probably end up dying with her purpose on the inside of her.

She really got involved in the ministry at her church, but she continued to struggle with not feeling good enough and that she didn't matter to anyone. She had so many walls up and chains to protect her from everyone, including God. She believed what God said, but she felt like it didn't apply to her because after all, she had never mattered to anyone. Most of her relationships were based upon what she was able to do for people, and she made sure she gave all she had in hopes of earning a place in someone's life. As soon as she was rejected, it just caused thicker walls and increased chains.

So, I'll share about her story at different times, but the first step in her turnaround began with prayer, and lots of prayer. We must pray and ask God to begin breaking the chains off our minds. The songwriter states that there is power in the name of Jesus to break every chain. You must give it to Jesus daily and ask Him to break the chains. It's a daily process; the Word of God tells us that we are to renew our minds daily. We are also instructed to take every thought and imagination captive. If you want to discover and truly believe that you matter, put into practice daily to change your thoughts; you do it through prayer and reading the Word.

God has so much purpose in His creation and we are all part of His creation. God is in the details of life. You'll see it as you look at the detail that went into the creation of the Earth and other planets. He considered every detail of how the sunset would rise and set. He considered the oceans and the clouds and the purpose they have to the Earth. He considered every organ in the human body when He created us in His image, and He considered every aspect of your personality and every life experience. He knew every hurtful event that would take place in your life. So, it's important as His creation that you go back to your Creator and find out what your purpose is and allow Him to heal you of every hurt and disappointment. Ask God to show you everything that you are still holding on to that is hindering you from seeing your true worth, because you matter, and you matter in a powerful way. This is your season to allow God to break the chains off your mind and heart; this is your time to heal completely.

Intentional Living

We're officially more than three months into 2020 and dealing with a pandemic that has caused all of us to review our priorities and determine what really matters! But without question, this time of year seems to be the most productive for people. I went to my gym in January and it was packed. Not unlike myself, most folks have motivational inspirational quotes plastered on their walls, phones, and computers. We have pledged to become better people this year and we have also started a new diet. What an exciting time to be surrounded by motivated people declaring a new journey toward personal improvement. But the reality is, the inspirational quotes no longer inspire and are covered up with pictures or more pressing issues. Sadly, in about two more weeks our diets will succumb to burgers and fries, super-sized, because good intentions alone just don't work. See, good intentions without a consistent plan of action is merely a great idea. You and I looked at the coming New Year and said, "Yeah! A new day, a New Year; it's my time to start over! This year I will do something new with my problems and issues!" Our declarations push our good intentions to take that first step, like when I went to the gym. If my intentions are strong, I might be able to squeeze out a few steps and work out three weeks in a row. I am doing great! Right? Sadly, my good intentions don't last. Our culture is great for inspiring good intentions but is less supportive of being and living intentionally. There is a gap as wide as the Grand Canyon between having good intentions and living intentionally. The *Merriam-Webster* dictionary describes *good intentions* as an: *aim, dream, idea, goal, wish, desire, and hope.* In other words, hopefully, someday, a daily dream; does this sound familiar? Is it how you describe your intentions? Now let's look at words great leaders use to describe their intentionality: action plans, purpose, definitely, and today. All these words are action words and speak to right now, in the moment; today I am committed to do …! People who utilize these words get things done; they are people who live their lives intentionally. Intentional living has nothing to do with age or station in life; it has to do with a resolution to get things done now! Have you noticed with yourself and others you know, we give up on workouts, diets, and self-improvement, most of our earlier motivation falling by the wayside? But what if your point of reference changed for the same activity? What if your intentional living was focused on making a difference in someone else's life? It doesn't matter if it's something huge or small; it just needs to touch someone other than you in a significant way. See, when our motivation is all about us, we will let ourselves off the hook too easily. You know when you grade yourself on a curve, it's either pass or fail. The secret is to shift the focus from yourself, or just your success, to creating something positive from your issue that benefits others. For example, what if you turned your diet into a challenge with friends to join in, and whoever loses X amount of weight wins the prize? What if working smarter or harder for yourself turned into making your office a better place for everyone else? This is intentional living, everyday actions based on making changes or making a difference in someone else's life. What's your goal for the New Year? Is it to embrace your significance? Is it to begin walking in your destiny as a person that matters? Both are great starts but why not take some time to see how you can focus your efforts on someone else. If you can change your focus by including others, I promise your smallest efforts will launch you into completing your goals with exponential success.

> *"No man can get rich himself unless he enriches others."*
> **— Earl Nightingale, The Strangest Secret**

I am challenging you to move your growth forward by leaps and bounds by embracing others in your process. By doing this, you change your life by changing the lives of others. The investment you make in them will pay you personal dividends into eternity. Intentional living demands personal growth, neither happens automatically. This process takes a plan. It's not just any plan but one that's strategic, specific, and time-centered. Motivational speaker Earl Nightingale said, "If a person will spend one hour per day on the same subject for five years, that person will be an expert on that subject." This statement tells us how far we can go when we have the discipline to make growth a daily practice. Intentional living puts into practice disciplines that produce the fruit of life. If you are planning for growth you must set a daily time to work toward that end. Going to the next level demands that you take personal responsibility for continuing your growth. It never ceases to amaze me how people can spend years in school being challenged to learn, then graduate and never open another book. Next-level growth is not automatic; it will take intentional planning to go to the next level. We can discern a person's success because it is determined by their daily agenda. Don't discount yourself and your growth; schedule your time intentionally for personal growth. I mean, put it on your calendar. Never allow your zeal for change to take the place of strong discipline connected to your plan. To support sustained growth, it must be scheduled. To begin, you must find out what your passions are because finding your passions will lead you to your natural talents. Once you have pinpointed them you can begin working diligently to develop those talents into extraordinary skills. Start by concentrating on your strengths, work them, and fine-tune them so they become more than just good, or above average but they excel to excellent. This is a greater beginning than undergirding your weaknesses. When you stray or allow others to pull you from your strengths, it puts negativity into motion for you and others working with you. Make a practice to include in your inner circle, movers and shakers, passionate people who keep your fire lit. Stay away from people who are just 'chillin' with nothing to do and no place to go. Make your association's fellow learners, people connected to your strength. Watch them and learn as they promote their personal growth. You will find them using techniques to strengthen their strengths, which you will likewise, just by association. Do the same with yours. In addition to connecting to the right people, do your research on the area you want to improve. When you find really great content that strikes you; file it away for future reference and use. Passionate, intentional people are readers;

they hunger and thirst for insights and understanding when they come across new knowledge. All the above recommendations are of no help if you're not prepared to apply them to your life. Application is the key. I learned a practice early, while working on my business degree, which is called the 24-hour rule. It states every time you learn something significant you share it with someone else within 24 hours. The premise is if you fail to apply this new knowledge to your life or to share it with someone else, you'll lose the lesson. Constant growth is the great separator of those who succeed and those who do not. Decide right now to become a lifelong learner. It is the only way your personal growth is guaranteed. Personal growth is not like your physical height; it is in your control; you can do something about it. Now that should cause you to sigh with relief! Everyone can grow and improve. It is in your hands to grow or not grow based on your level of commitment. You will be on your way to becoming all that matters to you. This will happen for you by being disciplined along with constant and continuous learning. Instituting this regime into your life will ensure you will be growing every day over the course of many years. You will amaze yourself once you begin this process. Moving from a life of arbitrary living where you have taken life as it comes, living each day wondering what's going to happen next, and reaching for only what will benefit you won't be easy. I am suggesting that you begin to look outside to heal your inside. You had to take the time to assess what was causing you to devalue your worth and value. Now that you have come to grips with the wilderness you have existed in for all these years, it's now time for you to command your moments into the successful person you were created to be. Begin by being more aware of your purpose daily;

don't wait for your day to emerge but set the time you plan to embrace your present, which is today! Think on purpose or intentionally about your day and what you will accomplish every day. Seek truth and authenticity with all relationships; be cautious in connecting with anyone not adding value to your day. This means either by what they bring to you, or by what you are providing to them. Do an attitude check on yourself making sure you put others first in value, love, and belief in their potential. This is the only way to truly measure your success. What matters and what is of value is what you put your potential and focus on every day. Never accept your life as it is. Don't allow negative situations to lead you by the nose. Instead, lead your life; improve your potential; and engage in growth. Intentionally live past the pain by purposefully challenging everything that's holding you back, and willfully embracing the newness of change.

Plugging into the right connection

Working with a skewed talent pool that was constantly increasing and falling off based on their charges and the release dates, did not diminish the completive drive of their coach. Ed Cheltenham, head coach of Spring Mountain Youth Camp's basketball team has an undying will to win. With his coaching, his teams seldom did anything else. Coach Ed was a probation officer at the juvenile correction facility based on top of Mt. Charleston, NV. He has, for over 33 years, worked with juvenile delinquents who were incarcerated for various degrees of charges. The biggest challenge was that most of them had never played the game or if they played, it was "street ball," which means they had no concept of playing on a team or even how to be loyal to a team. Most of these young men were able to survive into their teens by taking care of number one, every man for himself, dog-eat-dog attitudes. So, Coach Ed had his work cut out for him. He was armed with a keen eye of seeing diamonds in the raw and had a cunning evaluation of possible talent. His brilliance in teaching basketball skills to a rag-tag group of misfits seemed to rise as his fine suit. Their success also spoke to a quality of attitude and behavior demanded by Coach Ed that rivaled the public and private school teams they played. While the former teams enjoyed returning players and grooming players from ninth through twelfth grade, Spring Mountain held young men from six to nine months. Every year he inherited this same type of talent that the local basketball media prophets wrote off, if they mentioned them at all. Most would find this a daunting task, but Coach Ed was a winner and he knew how to plug into the right connections. Although his coaching techniques seem harsh, overly corrective as he demanded discipline, the onlookers were astonished by the response of his team. They knew that although he was tough on the floor, he had balanced his competitive drive with a special personal connection. His team saw him as a caring leader, fatherly, and only looking after their good. They would argue you down insisting he was only concerned for each of them on a personal level. Coach Ed used time-tested skills while coaching to build relationships with each young man, supporting their individual needs. Coach Ed knew he couldn't just prepare these young men to win on the court; the greater task was to prepare them to win in life. He intentionally invested in the cohesiveness of the team taking time to celebrate everyone's achievement and allowing them to have fun together.

Although each team enjoyed winning seasons, it wasn't until the year 2015 that all of Coach Ed's work came to fruition. While at the Orleans Arena in Las Vegas, NV, his Cinderella team became the State Champions. Although the game was exciting and exhilarating, it was the faces of parents and family members that was most exciting as they watched their young men, who were slated to become nothing, running, crying, hugging and laughing as they took turns passing the golden vial, the winning trophy! It was a glimpse of Heaven.

Relationships determine the depth of your connections. By investing in them, you will in turn gain sustained energy and endurance as a team. Your investment provides a return if the connections are the right people, making the journey more enjoyable for everyone. You must ask yourself a question before you begin with people, are you ready to be involved with people, to put in the effort? If yes, it would mean you are willing and ready to focus on others. Until you can honestly reflect on these questions and know you are ready, you should not attempt to establish these types of relationships. Good relationships are built on an existing foundation geared to working toward achievement. It is imperative that you understand that relationships are not the end-all, but they are the foundation that everything else sits on. They are the concrete we need to pour to live successful, stable, and fulfilling lives. Most of us are guilty of taking our relationships for granted, thinking they will always be there, always be supportive and always help us out. It's not good to live this way, because everything in our lives revolves around our ability to build, sustain and develop healthy relationships. It is so true that developing people skills determines our potential success. All of us can learn and practice skills that make us great with people and help us succeed in almost everything that matters. Are you ready to become someone other people value? Are you ready to become someone others clamor to be around or connected to, because you understand the value of connecting to the right people? If so, this is for you. Don't just read the words but put them into action, "faith without works is dead!" It is a proven fact that because most of us grew up in dysfunctional families, it is almost impossible to build healthy relationships without getting help and learning new skills. It is impossible to reproduce what wasn't modeled for you in the first place. You cannot begin, maintain, and build healthy relationships if you have never been exposed to them. Many people are so self-centered and self-satisfying that others just don't matter to them. They never think of the needs of others nor do they seek to know them. Still others have been hurt, abused, and misused in their past and it causes them to be distrustful of everyone hindering their ability to connect and initiate good relationships. Because of these issues, many must begin learning themselves, healing broken places and gaining skills for reaching out to other people before relationships with others can be initiated. It takes relationally whole people to build and sustain good relationships. Two broken people do not equal a whole relationship! All of us see life through the lens of our own upbringing, experiences, and issues. It is what's on the inside that informs how we see the outside. Perception is reality for us, and it determines how we see others. My mother would say, "Some people see all people through their dysfunction." "If they're liars, they think everyone lies; if they are stealers, they think everyone steals. If they are not trustworthy, they believe no one is trustworthy." She would then say, "The opposite is true for healthy people; if they are loving, they expect love from others. If they are honest, they approach the world expecting everyone to be honest." In other words, our perspective comes from what we believe is true about ourselves. It stands to reason that we should not work hard at changing others. Our task is to change ourselves beginning with our point of view. If you do the work on yourself of becoming a person who truly matters, you in turn change how you see others. It never ceases to amaze me how we are willing to evaluate everyone else and pinpoint who they are and what their problems are, but we fail at doing the same for ourselves. Because of our unchecked and uncorrected dysfunctions, which has caused us to have a negative self-image, we are prone to establish and build unhealthy relationships. Without help to develop new skills and elevate our expectations, we all tend to bring ourselves down to the level of our own expectations. It is our responsibility to develop a personal culture of being a lifelong learner. There is nothing in life that you will be successful at if you do not throw your whole self at it. When we are on a journey to form great connections, we must be able to put our personal agendas aside for the purpose of building the relationships. When people enter your life and add value to your life, they do it intentionally, with calculated purpose, because adding value to someone else's life requires an investment from the giver. All of us understand that receiving is easy, and most folks want to be the recipient and not the giver. Working to be a positive influence in someone's life takes time, effort, and added value. People who elevate others practice this skill daily, knowing that their thoughts determine their words. As they discipline their thoughts, they simultaneously add encouraging words into their own lives so that sharing them with others flows easily from them.

Are you ready to make that connection?

In our attempt to build our self-worth and value as well as launch into making important relationship connections, we must "Eat the F.R.O.G." The F.R.O.G. is an acronym for:

F= Focus on who I am. Am I positive of who that is? Are you ready to focus on the relationship?

R= Review your issues; have you addressed all of them? Are you working or eliminating or dealing with them?

O= Others first. Are you willing to put another person's needs first? Are you disciplining yourself with organized thoughts and emotions? Are you telling yourself the truth? Are you giving yourself thoughtful encouragement?

G= Growth. Have you begun and maintained the process of self-improvement? Have you dazzled yourself on your achievements?

Eating the FROG is asking ourselves, "Am I ready to make a great connection?" Don't answer too fast; now slowly bite into the truth! For this new revelation we must eat the F.R.O.G. one bite at a time. Begin this self-examination one letter (bite) at a time until you have eaten your frog. By working through this, you know whether you have built a personal foundation sound enough to support any connection. So, let's eat this FROG!

I believe that issues on the inside always show on the outside so we must begin asking ourselves questions before we can reach out to pull others into our worlds. Focusing on the inside means looking at your emotional health, spiritual health, and then your life demands. Have you established self-disciplines that build on the You God has created you to be? Do you begin your day with an ordered plan? Do you always start with quiet time, meditating on God? These are the first steps of beginning to build a solid foundation. The Bible says, "A wise man builds his house on a rock." (Matthew 7:24) Anything other than truth, which is rock solid, will crumble and fall when excessive pressure is placed on it. Taking the time to focus on what has hindered you in the past from establishing and maintaining healthy relationships and dealing with those things, moves you closer to relationship readiness. When you address and handle the hurts you have hidden all these years, past hurts will cease to be the source all your relationships evolve around. Because when you lead from your hurts and deal with people out of your emotions, the result is hurting people always hurt people. Then the people you hurt in turn damage your sensitive emotions. By focusing on them, you pull the bandage off and expose your hurting issues to the air and light of truth, and just like my Grandma said, "Things covered don't heal and things exposed to good air and the light of God always heal!" If the hurt is too deep to do this by yourself, then find a trustworthy friend or counselor to help you through this healing process. As you complete the F process and open wide to take a big bite into the R, you will notice that when you were focusing on your issues you have also reviewed what's going on with you. The greater, richer part of eating the R of your FROG, is creating a personal improvement plan, something that challenges the who you used to be and ushers you toward the person God called you to be.

Personal improvement plans can be a list of goals connected to the direction or growth you would like to accomplish and how you want to measure your success with those goals. The goals can range from checking yourself about negative thoughts and words, to losing weight, learning a new task, gaining a degree, or applying for a new job. Whatever your list may contain, it should be things important to you, things you desire, not a list from someone else. Also, connecting an accountability partner into your plan will ensure your success. A strong supportive circle is a key factor to being successful. Most of us do very well with these types of plans because they provide clear serious directions about what you need to do to obtain your goals. Since this plan is created by you and for you, it is a reminder of where you plan to be within a reasonable amount of time. If done right, it should not be the rule of your life but a guide to obtain desired goals. The moment the plan becomes a task master, you have taken it out of context and should be stopped immediately. It is not suggested or designed to put further burden on you when you're struggling to come from under issues that have weighed you down, but you also don't want to make positive moves and stop without moving toward what your vision is for your life. Having something that encourages movement is what I am suggesting here. Our next bite is the O, the sweet spot of the donut if you will! It is the letter or move that speaks to relationships. Are you ready to consider the other person first? Are you ready to put some of the things you want in favor of the person you're building a relationship with? Friendships, whether it's with a male or female, takes time and sacrifice. Selfish people don't do well in relationships, especially healthy ones. Healthy relationships begin with both parties being sound within themselves, not looking for someone to complete them or make them better but their focus is to make that person better. We look for the good in that person allowing it to overshadow any flaws we may see, if the flaws don't cause us harm, physically, emotionally or spiritually. Most folks are drawn to people who show interest in them. They may pursue for a little while but sooner rather than later, they will give up if that person doesn't show the slightest interest in them. Remember, we are discussing healthy people. When people hurt or disappoint you, and they will, instead of ending the relationship or giving them a piece of your mind, you take a piece of their mind trying to understand their vantage point, their point of view, understanding we can learn something from everyone, even children. Since you are practicing believing and speaking the best about you, applying this principle to others opens the door for you to speak encouraging words to them. These positive affirmations bring people close to each other. It allows you to believe the best about them and them to believe the same about you. Your growth changes will allow you to care for others and therefore you become slow to engaging in conflict with them. How healthy people deal with conflict is very different from people who are unhealthy due to emotional issues. Every relationship has its conflicts; it's a natural process of life but knowing how to effectively use conflicts to engage in productive communication is the key. Mismanaged conflict only harms relationships. All conflict must be handled in a respectful and positive way. Conflict can provide an opportunity for growth and can assist in developing and ultimately strengthening the bond between people. As you know, conflicts arise when people see things differently. When people disagree over what they value and what motivates them, they can also conflict over perceptions, ideas and or desires. Many times, the conflict is small over small things but sometimes there are deep strong feelings or unresolved issues at the core of the problems. It is important when a conflict arises that you keep in mind that both of you have a need to feel safe, secure, and respected. It may seem strange, but people can conflict out of one's need for greater closeness and intimacy. Yes, it seems counterproductive to be in conflict when you want to be close. But if the other person doesn't value that need, it causes conflict, which ultimately damages communication and could end the relationship. It is so important that we realize when we believe and try to see the best in people, that's usually what comes from them. Most of our confrontations will diminish if we remember how much we care for others; these types of thoughts will override conflict.

The Right Tools to Build Trust

One of the most important tools of trust is to be able to trust yourself. If you are unable to depend on yourself, relationships cannot begin for you. It is not dealing in integrity and truth when you establish relationships based on a promise of trust and you cannot trust yourself. When people have made too many mistakes and bad choices, they find it hard to trust themselves, especially with truly important things. Others think nothing of living a life of lying. They lie to themselves to make them look or feel good. They choose lying when they are unsure of what others may think and feel. It is near impossible to trust someone you know practices lying. I have heard of people who tell their children to say they are not home when someone is at the door or on the phone. They give no thought to what they are teaching their children in the long run. These sorts of things are clear illustrations of someone who does not trust themselves. Once you have gone through the process of restoring your self-trust you will find strength of character and hope for life. How you treat, love, understand and enjoy yourself daily speaks to your current level of self-trust. This is intricately connected to you believing in your innate value and worth. Are your personal voices still sending negative, self-rejecting messages that you have accepted since childhood? Do you do things only for the approval of others? Is your value or performance tied to their opinions of you? Do you only feel safe when you're in control? Do you compare your choices with those made by others, even when you go out to eat? Are others' needs more important than yours to the point of you denying your personal needs? Do you find it difficult to recognize or tell the truth because it's been easier to lie to yourself? In our present world of technology, we are bombarded with information on how to improve ourselves; you have heard them. '10 steps to lose 10 pounds, 15 steps to a great love life, 25 proven steps to grow old rich,' and on and on they go! When you lack self-trust, you will try everyone's remedy and, unfortunately, never get to what you really want in life. Getting past the noise takes perseverance of character. Building your self-trust begins with building your character by developing personal integrity. Stephen M. R. Covey wrote an excellent book called the *The Speed of Trust: The One Thing That Changes Everything*. Covey states, "*Integrity is more than honesty (telling the truth); it is also leaving the right impression. There are three qualities: congruence, humility and courage. Think of congruence as having no gap between intent and behavior; it is walking the talk.*" Because our thoughts promote our actions, there is a direct connection between our level of integrity and our actions. While building your character to gain self-trust your mixture of virtues must be sprinkled with humility or grace, which enables us to not think more highly of ourselves than we should, and at the same time it assists us in finding the good in everyone. In the above book, it asserts that humility is being more concerned with what is right than being right. It also strengthens us to act out what is right by accepting correction from the truth on faulty or stinking thinking. Finally, in finding self-trust we must have courage to silence old negative voices from your childhood, as well as the courage to do what's right in the face of those condemning stares. Self-trust is built on what you know to be true about yourself. That truth is based on your abilities, talents, trainings, personality, and style. Knowing for sure what's in your toolbox gives you the ability to live with integrity trusting yourself. So how do I show others I'm trustworthy enough to establish healthy relationships? Others are also concerned or watching your behavior. Unfortunately, people judge our behavior, not what you intended to do. Unless they know us well, they really can't judge our heart, so they are left to judge our behavior. We begin building trustful relationships by speaking truth in love. This means talking straight, not having hidden agendas. Stepping toward people out of self-love and trust causes you to treat them with care and respect, which tells that person your expectations of how you would like to be treated. Speak honestly and openly about the topics covered by both of you. Things that should not be revealed, should not be brought up. But if something does come up in the conversation that you're not comfortable discussing, express your reservations openly and as honestly as you can. If the person you are building the relationship with is a person of integrity like you, they will respect your boundaries and believe you are a person worthy of their trust. As your relationship progresses, you should grow more transparent with each encounter until when you talk with each other, you opt for transparency and disclosure rather than being closed and distant. The thing that keeps this type of trust going is exercising the art of forgiveness. Yes, but to rebuild broken trust it takes more than saying "I'm sorry!" It takes making restitution. Restitutions are based on who the relationship is with and what they value. It means the offender must go the extra mile to mend what has been broken. For those who have shattered the trust of others it will take time and patience to rebuild what was done. However, through acts of restitution from the offender, the relationship can mend itself with work and if both parties are working toward that end.

Often the simple act of loyalty to the person and to the relationship will help ensure trust isn't broken.

CHAPTER FIVE

MY SPIRIT SET FREE

"So think of it this way: if the Son comes to make
you free, you will really be free."
— **(John 8:36, VOICE)**

We have talked about taking the chains off our minds so that we can begin to see that we really do matter in life.

Well, we must also allow our spirit to be free in order to come to full understanding that we matter. Our spirit can only be free by faith and faith comes by hearing the Word of God. Also, for your spirit to be free, there must be an agreement between your mind and your spirit. We can have an intellectual understanding of being free, but until we know it in our spirit, we will be bound.

So, how does our spirit come into agreement with our mind? It happens during getting to know God in an intimate way. We must spend time in worship and seeking His face and getting to know Him in a deep intimate way. God desires an intimate relationship with us. As you get to know Him and truly begin to love Him based on nothing more than Who He is, His love will overtake you. It's going to take you deciding that you want to experience God in an intimate way.

Intimacy is built through worship and prayer, not just by you talking, but also sitting quietly and allowing God to talk to you and pour His love on you. It's His love that will fill that longing

in your heart to be loved. It's His love that will heal every hurt that has rested in your heart and spirit.

It's God's love that will touch the very things that have caused you to not feel like you matter. Think about Who God is. He's the Creator of the universe, and you can look around at the Earth and see His craftsmanship. It's that very God that wants you to know Him intimately. He wants to spend quality time with you. He wants to show you where He's been in every situation in your life.

Imagine God with His arms open and imagine yourself laying in His lap and you can hear His heartbeat. There's nothing more intimate than that image and that's what God wants with YOU. He wants to reveal Himself to you in ways you can't imagine. If this is what God wants with you, how could you possibly not matter?

God knew you before He formed you in your mother's womb; that's what His Word says. He knew exactly what He had planned for you and He knew what needed to happen in order to accomplish His will and get glory out of your life.

God wants to spend time with you, and I can promise you that any time spent with God will never be a waste of time. You must make up your mind today that you will spend time with God in an intimate place.

There is a longing in your spirit to be whole. There is a longing in your spirit that wants to be free. There is a longing in your spirit that wants to be healed. There is a longing in your spirit that wants to be loved, and it was placed there by God to be filled with Him and only Him. He wants to fill whatever you need in your life.

As you read this book, please know that God has even ordained this in your life because He cares so much for you to make sure you know your value to Him and this world. Let me share a bit more of the testimony of the woman that I've began sharing with you. This woman's self-esteem was so low because of all the rejection that she experienced. She had an aunt that provided her with stability in her life, and while her aunt made every effort to make up for what her parents didn't do in her life, there was still a downfall even at her aunt's home. Her aunt and uncle, who also played the role of her godmother and godfather, loved her dearly, but her godfather was an alcoholic and her godmother ended up being an enabler as a result. Her godfather had converted the garage at their home into a sort of lounge. It had a television and a full bar, but it also had pornography everywhere. There were pornographic pictures hanging on the wall, and magazines on the tables. This was also the place where this woman, as a little girl, played with friends in the neighborhood. Unfortunately, it was also the place she was molested as a young girl. She never told her aunt what happened because she was afraid she would get in trouble. So, she held onto that secret. This young girl was in a position that she held several secrets. She held the secret that her father would beat up her mother. She held the secret that she was being molested by a friend of the family that she played with on a regular basis. Can you imagine what it was like to hold those secrets during her childhood? Can you imagine what it was like to hold such things because she was afraid of getting into trouble? Her spirit was far from free because it was holding on to ultimate betrayals.

So, how did she finally get to a place where her spirit could be free? She learned the importance of forgiveness and she learned the importance of being healed. She learned that in order to be

free in her spirit, she needed to allow God into those very places in her heart, because God was there with her when they happened and He was the one that wiped the tears when she cried in her bed as a child, not able to share what was going on. She learned that God had a plan for her life and that those very things she experienced could help others in need of a deep emotional healing. She learned that through spending time in God's Word and in worship that she was able to touch God and allow Him to touch her back. It was in worship that her spirit was healed and set free.

God wants to set your spirit free. This can happen when you make the decision to forgive who you need to forgive, including yourself. Now, allow God's love to heal you by spending time in prayer and worship consistently. Set aside time to listen to worship music. Set aside time to turn off the television and just allow worship music to play some evenings. Each moment you spend with God just loving on Him and allowing Him to love on you, will cause you to experience a new level of freedom in your spirit. Before you know it, you will look forward to getting away to be alone with God. No longer will you have to seek people and things to fill those places designed only to be filled by God. The day will come when you are so in love with God and so content with His love that nothing that has happened in your life will matter, because you know that in place of the pain, God has chosen you to be used for His glory.

God values exactly who you are, and He accepts you and everything about your personality. He's the one that created you and designed your life and He loves you for every quirk, every

insecurity and everything that you think is wrong with you. He has designed a plan to use, and He made you uniquely, and experienced every trial with you because He knew you would come to this point in your life where you would need to know how important you are to Him. If you look at your experiences that you felt were tragic and unfair, just know you are not alone; it wasn't your fault and you didn't cause any of it. Understand that there are others who have gone through similar situations and didn't live to tell their story. You survived, and you have a testimony. God protected you through the storms of life and you're here in your right mind and breath in your body, so you must know that you are valued.

If you need one more reassurance that God finds you valuable, here it is...He died to save **YOUR** life. If you were the only person on the planet, He still would have chosen to die for you. The Lord has declared and pronounced freedom over your life; Christ died to make that possible. The mystery is that it is your choice; He will not force freedom on you. The Bible says, *"Christ has set us free to live a free life. So take your stand! Never again let anyone put a harness of slavery on you."* *(Galatians 5:1, MSG)* In our day and age, the thought of slavery is like watching an old movie; it just doesn't seem real that someone can be in slavery today. But we are not talking about physical chains around someone's arms, ankles, or neck. I am suggesting that people can have total control over your emotions and behavior without touching you physically. Meet LaShawn, a beautiful young woman with two children, and Steve, her husband. LaShawn and her family were new to their local church. They joined one summer, on a Sunday morning, after Pastor Smith delivered an excellent message with the usual rhythmic cadence, accompanied by the soulful singing of the choir. LaShawn felt as if angels came to church that Sunday, just so

her family would know they were in the right place. Steve and LaShawn joined wholeheartedly. She began by getting involved with the women's department, working alongside one of the founding Mothers of the church, the stout matronly, over-nurturing, Mother Katherine Jones. LaShawn soon found herself being controlled by this sweet Mother Jones. Mother Jones told her how to pray prayers that she knew God would hear. She taught LaShawn acceptable songs to sing and how to think. She advised LaShawn on how to dress becoming of their church. It didn't take long for LaShawn's desire to please to be totally overtaken by Mother Jones' spirit of control. Soon she couldn't do anything in the church without Mother Jones' approval. LaShawn, from the time she was a little girl, felt the call of God to work as a missionary and to speak or teach other women. But Mother Jones disapproved and tried to hold LaShawn to what she wanted her to be. When people call you to a position, you are bound by their call, but when God calls you to your place, you are free to discover who you really are! LaShawn's will was surrendered to this Mother who took advantage of her need to please others. It took God and a friend praying with her to break this stronghold. She is now free to be all that God has called her to be. How about you? Who's controlling your life, your will, your destiny? If it's anyone other than God, you have given them too much power over you. When LaShawn accepted the freedom God has given, her spirit was set free. She received the power to hear what God intended for her and who she really was in Him. Her community mission work took off as she impacted the lives of women around her.

The apostle John teaches that, *"There is no fear in love. But perfect love drives out fear"* (1 John 4:18, *NIV*). When we realize that God's love is perfect, which means He loves you based on

Who He is and not on who you are trying to be. He loves your weaknesses, pain, confusion, and dysfunctions; none of these things will ever cause Him to not love you perfectly. Because He is the great exchange artist, in these weaknesses He exchanges them for His strength. When you get that in your spirit, you no longer fear acceptance because you finally understand you are accepted in the Beloved, fully and completely. The perfection of His love for you fills every empty space, elevates low self-worth, and fills your love tank! His perfect love causes you to walk in victory for every battle life throws at you. Now this is life abundantly because there is nothing impossible to those who believe.

Being really free is more than just a word; it's more than a comment. It is more than doing the usual from one week to the next. It is a journey in your mind and spirit to imagine the unimagined, to color outside the lines, to finally realize that who God says you are is more than you have been working on, more than you can think or imagine, and costing more than you can pay. I know, I know, you say this elephant is just too large! How do you eat this elephant, or eat the whole roll of the Bible? I respond just as others have stated before me; you eat an elephant one bite at a time. You answer your God-Sized Call one step at a time, for the steps of righteous people are ordered by the Lord. Remember, He orders your steps, not your stride! That's why some folks are further along than others. They took the freedom call of God and hit the ground running, remembering to step where He steps, listening intently to His still small voice of where your next step may be. Although God has your entire life mapped out, He wants you to trust His direction, and gain every ounce of power along the journey. You do this by doing what David said in Psalm 34: 1-8 (*MSG*)

> [1] *I bless* GOD *every chance I get;*
> *my lungs expand with his praise.*
>
> [2] *I live and breathe* GOD;
> *if things aren't going well, hear this and be happy:*
>
> [3] *Join me in spreading the news;*
> *together let's get the word out.*
>
> [4] GOD *met me more than halfway,*
> *he freed me from my anxious fears.*
>
> [5] *Look at him; give him your warmest smile.*
> *Never hide your feelings from him.*
>
> [6] *When I was desperate, I called out,*
> *and* GOD *got me out of a tight spot.*
>
> [7] GOD's *angel sets up a circle*
> *of protection around us while we pray.*
>
> [8] *Open your mouth and taste, open your eyes and see—*
> *how good* GOD *is. Blessed are you who run to him.*

There is awesome power in your 'Yes' to God, even when you are not sure how to say Yes. God rarely reveals where He is ultimately taking you, but your willingness to run to Him diminishes the power of your fears and weakness to accomplish what seemed to be impossible for you. It all lands on trust. Trust can keep you buoyant in the ocean of life. Trust fills the cracks and crevices in your belief system to help you rise to the occasion or call. Before you leap, you must trust you will rise. The ability to rise is not in your need to leap, but it is in putting all your trust in the One Who can keep you from falling. That single act of applying your will and behavior to trusting that God's will is to help you succeed, is all you need to turn your life around. The act of trust turns relationships around and causes them to become a force for the world to reconcile with. The Bible says, *"The fundamental fact of existence is that this trust in God, this faith, is the firm foundation under everything that makes life worth living. It's our handle on what we can't see. The act of faith is what distinguished our ancestors, set them above the crowd."* (Hebrews11:1, 2, *MSG*).

The fundamental fact of faith changes everything! The act of faith speaks to the ability to apply trust in places, circumstances, and people when there is no evidence that it's deserved, earned or warranted. Our eyesight helps us by clearly bringing into focus things in our world. The same is true with faith in the unseen, and the spiritual world. Faith pulls into our vision evidence of what's there and that it is available to us. Trust through faith has its boundaries. I'm not talking about some blind jump off a cliff, calling it faith. Faith is understood through the spirit alone. It is more than what you sense or feel. It's not something that others can determine or measure by some external test. Faith has its roots in trust and trust gains its growth in faith. So, the ability to trust is needed to work, live and to become successful in our world. It allows us to believe what's not readily seen. Trust is not in conflict with reason or your mind, but trust can confound reason and leave logic questioning. So, faith is not just believing, and it is not the understanding of the intellect. It is an act or a willingness to trust, to move, and to work with the things we cannot see.

Value, Worth, Costs

What does Value mean? My dictionary says "The regard that something is held to deserve; the importance, worth, or usefulness of something. (To) consider (someone or something) to be important or beneficial; have a high opinion of."(Oxford Dictionary) The Bible indicates your value is based on the actions and feelings of God and it says: "For God so loved the world, that he gave his only begotten Son, that whosoever believeth in him (Jesus) should not perish, but have everlasting life." (John 3:16).

So, value equals worth which also drives the cost of what's valued. When we begin our quest for finding value in ourselves, our first lesson is learning how to have a relationship with our self. It is imperative that you understand you can choose to be your own best friend or your own worst enemy. It really doesn't matter how many people, fans, friends or family you may have or who may attend your important events. You are always present, the number one guest on your life list. Your self-worth must be honest and healthy for your well-being to be intact. Self-value is not the same as self-esteem, although people use them interchangeably. Self-esteem has its roots in confidence and a sense of well-being and admiration for yourself.

But valuing one's self is the lips, hips, and tips of the lady, or the lips, eyes, and muscles of the man! It's the mental and emotional care taken that leads to a healthy self. Not having self-worth initiates the suffering of self. Since self-value grows from the inside of us, it is the part of us that we alone control. That means that you determine who deposits or withdraws from your sense of value/worth. They are the people or things, like our loved ones and jobs, that we have given permission to gain entry into our emotional bank. Some folks are extremely open to external voices, who set standards, rules, and boundaries. When you live a life run by external sources, you are basing your self-worth on a risky slippery slope. These sources tend to change at will and many of the people in your source groups suffer from low self-worth themselves. Being sure your hope is built on no one less than Jesus Christ and right living will ensure your life is built on the things essential for a strong internal foundation. Finding value in yourself is coming to grips with the knowledge of you being one of a kind, and it's impossible to compare yourself to others, because there is no one like you. It would be like comparing apples to oranges. Both are fruit; however, they are not even close to being the same. Some may say the orange is better because it's full of juice and citrusy. Others may say the apple is better because it's firm, sweet and full of fiber. The comparison makes no sense because the two fruits are not the same. This applies to you and anyone you might compare yourself to. What you would be doing is living by their value standards instead of your own. Using the standards of others for yourself is the best way to overlook your personal accomplishments, goals, and achievements. Others will celebrate you when you won't celebrate yourself, because you have not set a personal standard which is most important to your well-being in the long run. Build your standards on higher things like being balanced in your life, being kind to others and having a firm faith foundation. Next, learn the art of failing forward by embracing mistakes, mishaps, and miss-steps. Most of us struggle with thoughts of our mistakes. These thoughts bring anxiety, fear, regret, and shame. There is no way to go back and change those mistakes; hindsight is the best sight. But we can control or change how we view our mistakes. Instead of seeing yourself as a total failure, change your viewpoint to seeing your mistakes as a learning experience. Develop self-directed questions so you discover what caused the mistakes, empowering you to make necessary changes, so you don't repeat the same issue over and over again. The next step you must take is to embrace being an ever-learner, consistently seeking opportunities to improve who you are as well as elevate your possibilities. Engage in groups with like-minded people; attend conferences, workshops, or lectures. Learn a hobby even if you don't have time. Meditate, read, love and pray. Whatever you take on has awesome possibilities of lifting your self-esteem which will improve your self-worth. Take time to gain a mentor, someone you can share your struggles and your journey with; someone who can help you establish goals to move forward; someone that will help frame your thoughts to keep you connected to your point of faith and bring you back to the standards you have established, which lifts the real you. Include this in your growth journey; offer to help someone else by giving yourself to others. This simple act offers great rewards for you and for them. It also helps you to not overly focus on the negative things in your life, but pull you toward positive empowering moments. Finally, no matter where you are in your journey, embrace the quest for self-worth because it is a never-ending battle. You can do this by keeping your emotional, mental, and spiritual closet clean of all clutter, so there is room for growth to help you maintain a healthy sense of value and self-worth. You can never do anything greater or more honorable than working to lift and improve how you see yourself, which lifts your self-value. It is impossible to lift others if we have not taken the time to lift ourselves. You may encourage them to a point; however, if your encouragement isn't from a strong place within yourself, the soft elevation doesn't hold. You will find that they have become more dependent on your consistent words instead of on their strength gained from a word of life-giving encouragement. This type of encouragement becomes a seed that takes root that causes them to lift their own personal self-worth. Knowing, understanding, and developing your own personal value and worth is the catalyst for your success. The ability to trust who you are and your potential to become all that you believe, enables others to give you this same level of trust. This remarkable exchange between yourself and others is the groundwork for exceptional growth, potential wealth, and believability. This is the cost of who you are; it is the measure of who you shall become as well as the legacy you leave for those who follow you. It is your life journey to ensure that you experience continued growth and well-being. Personal investment always costs you something that includes your time, talent, positions, and behavior. All of these must be offered on the altar of self-growth in order to become all that God has created you to be. The bill of building self-value is giving to everyone but only those striving for bigger and better will pay the daily cost of becoming just what they see!

Working inside strengthens outside

In 2015, Pixar created an animated movie called Inside Out, which deals with the conflicting emotions of a young girl. The main character is Riley and like all of us, Riley is guided by her emotions. Joy, Fear, Anger, Disgust and Sadness are the emotions shown in the movie. Like all emotions, these emotions live in Headquarters, the control center inside Riley's mind, where they help advise her through everyday life. As Riley and her emotions struggle to adjust to a new life in San Francisco, turmoil ensues in Headquarters. Although Joy, Riley's main and most important emotion, tries to keep things positive, the emotions conflict on how best to navigate a new city, house, and school.

Not unlike Riley, we too have primary emotions that advise us through our days. Likewise, our primary emotion works on our behalf. For example, if a negative emotion is dominating us, that primary emotion controls our behavior. In that case, we can work on that primary emotion giving us the ability to change our emotional makeup, so we become the successful person were striving to be. To make that change, there are five areas of growth that I would like you to concentrate on, and they too live in the headquarters of your mind. These areas can complement each other, or they can conflict if you don't use them for your growth. In building ourselves, it boils down to developing *value, worth, believability, behavior and use of time*. In the previous chapter, I spoke about your value and worth, so I want to spend some time talking about what you believe and your outward believability. It's important that we always have a sound healthy belief system . The Bible teaches that we should let the mind of Christ live inside of us, which means bringing every thought and idea into alignment with what Christ taught and lived. Otherwise, one of two stimuli will influence us, altering our path. Stimuli is internal and/or external pressures. While under these influences they can keep you in a negative nonproductive place. When you are unsure of your own belief system you are unable to complete your life journey, and the consequences can be you end up living and going in circles around the same set of issues and problems.

Most folks live ignoring or taking their belief systems for granted. They sail through life hoping to navigate life's ocean making it to the proverbial shore. While that approach might work for a while, you will ultimately find your life empty, without substance, and wondering what you need to do to get on track. A healthy belief system gives you a foundation for true self-value and self-worth that can be used to base everything you do, say, or establish in your life.

We can classify our value or worth as a 'set of rules' or boundaries that define how we process and store information. This "set of rules" also establishes how we behave and sets rules for our expectations of the behavior of others. Since we have this base of knowledge from which to function, we can easily go out and find the answers to our questions to fill in the gaps that this new, unknown information created. But, without any rules, new information is just tossed into the corners of our minds. Without God-centered rules, it can cause confusion and a fight our self-esteem. This flood of ideas and thoughts can push the information to our conscious mind, overloading its ability to organize that information, based on the rules of order for your life. The conscious mind devises a set of questions that need to be answered in order to make sense of what it has been exposed to. As these questions float unattended by sound rules in our mind, they can cause frustration, fear, and sometimes an overwhelming depression leaving you feeling that life is imploding on you.

When you were born, you established rules and boundaries by your senses, hot, cold, soft, hard, bright, and dark. As you developed, you expanded those rules to include nice, funny, sad, and mad. This set of values worked while we were very young, but eventually you had to move forward in learning about people. You learned what makes people tick and what drives their behavior, as well as the world around you, which demands that we expand ourselves so that we can become all that we desire. In working to determine or renew your belief system, you must identify what you value, not what you like or what you choose but what you really value. This means what decisions are made in good times or bad times. To begin this process, spend time with your own thoughts determining what you hold as being dear to you. Is it family or friends, or your career? Or, is it other people or items that you deem important to you, or in some way defines who you are now and in the future?

This list of things you hold dear establishes your core. The foundation of everything you think is based on this core. Take a moment and write them down and explain why each one is important to you. This will help you clarify what's important in and for your life. The same is true when you have a faulty "set of rules" based on lies, deception and manipulation. Those rules may have been telling you that you have no value; no one will ever love you, and you will always be alone. You may be hearing more negative self-talk. These negative self-destructive rules must be redefined. The biggest problem is that most folks don't adjust their belief system as they grow. If you were raised in lack and want, everything in your life was about survival. The value rules centered on survival and rightly so. But now you are prosperous, and you've become a hoarder, self-centered or having consistent thoughts that others want to take things from you, because you did not redefine your core values. Every year you must assess and readjust your rules, especially if they fight you, and can't sustain you for the next level of life. We have to boldly get rid of old antiquated ideas and rules, rules from when we were 10, 11, or 12 years old being abused or molested by friend or family. Those rules are no longer necessary today now that you are in control of your life through Christ.

You must put new rules in place that align with where you're headed in life. This process can be difficult if you fear change. If that is the case, you must initiate positive self-talk to begin accepting that our set of rules will and should change over the course of your life. It is very important that you take control of that process inviting change to take its place in your mind. Remember, when setting your belief system, you must do this through conscious, rational, and logical thought. It is not feelings but rules that have a sure basis; they must begin with what you believe about God and your relationship with Him. Our hope is built on nothing less than Jesus Christ and His righteousness. On this sure foundation we live and move and have our being. If you are unsure of this, you cannot move forward until you establish a basis for the most important relationship in your life. By working through this area, you will better handle experiences and issues that come to hinder or stop you by comparing them to what you value most. Problems lose their potency when compared to the shadow of the Almighty and what you know for sure about Him.

Belief and faith run hand in hand; they are two sides of the same coin. Creators of the intersection between growth and answered prayers lies with these twins. The Bible says without faith (a belief system) it is impossible to please God (Hebrews 11:6) and without a belief system, it is impossible to live a healthy growing life. The Word of God (Bible) teaches that growing faith is not a struggle, it is a gift that comes from God through grace. It is so free! God gives it freely when we meet His conditions. What are the conditions? Glad you asked. Ephesians 2:8, 9 says it this way, "For it is by grace you have been saved, through faith—and this is not from yourselves, it is the gift of God—not by works, so that no one can boast." (*NIV*) Faith or belief is not something that we can think it into our lives outside the grace of God. That type of belief is weak and will only last for a short period. If your belief is purely based on emotion and your logic, then faith becomes something out of the depths of your own thoughts and not God's thoughts and Will toward you. When you concoct your own belief system outside of the Will of God, this type of faith is something that's believable to you but it does not come with the power and authority of faith you believed and received from God. Concocted faith is all in your mind and is not supported by God at all. The faith God gives is supernatural and establishes for you a strong cornerstone that your life belief systems can be added to. This faith is supernatural, spiritual, and impacts you personally as well as being vital to your everyday life and progress. Because it is from God it is alive and active, and it causes life and activity for those who receive faith in God in their hearts, minds, and spirits. This foundational faith comes by hearing and receiving God's Word in your heart. It will build your personal belief system. Begin building it by meditating on the Word of God until you know in the "City of your Soul" that you have heard from God. It is worth this effort because faith is the commerce of God. With faith comes the promises of God. With faith comes guidance, stability, trust, and believability.

Now that you have received and believed Who God is, it's time to discipline and focus your mind on seeking your own personal rules. Your personal set of rules for your belief system will help you gain an atmosphere where you trust yourself, your decisions, and your chosen direction for your life. It is now time to establish relationships based on trust and believability. Because you believe in your own ability to act it's time to approach all other encounters on the basis that you are a credible person; people can trust in you and your ability to follow through. When you have accepted God's faith in your life you project personal strength that others can believe in. This new beginning builds your self-confidence, which informs your self-worth, and extends them both exponentially.

"Self-trust is the first secret of success ... the essence of heroism."
— Ralph Waldo Emerson

Trying to build trust is easier said than done. Do you find it strange that you can often trust other people more than you trust yourself? All other people must do is look official and wear a white jacket and we'll allow them check places we won't allow loved ones to venture into. People can make a video on social media and claim to be the latest and greatest diet guru and we'll purchase their products for their "bubble gum diet." We will trust anyone and everyone before we trust our thoughts and decisions. If you check the *Miriam Online Dictionary* you will find the following synonyms for self-trust: *aplomb, assurance, self-assurance, self-assuredness, self-confidence, self-esteem.* Okay, are you as confused as I am as to what self-trust really looks like? Excuse my bluntness but what in God's name is *aplomb*? I guess it's not something you eat. Right? So, if you're going to develop this trait or increase your level of self-trust, we must dig a little deeper. Begin with self-examination. Being honest with yourself, would you say you have very low self-trust? Do you usually seek the opinion of others first before you make a move? Or would you say you have extreme self-trust and you rarely seek others for second opinions? If you are like most folks, you fluctuate between trusting your thoughts without the backup of others to the other extreme of being frozen in your thoughts until someone else qualifies your direction. Maya Angelou, the great speaker and poet said, "I do not trust people who don't love themselves and yet tell me, 'I love you.'" There is an African saying which is: "Be careful when a naked person offers you a shirt." An unknown speaker posed a question to a group of renowned leaders in business, finance, government and education. She asked, *"If you had to make an important decision and the information told you one thing but your*

intuition and gut strongly told you another, what would you do?"
Most of these great leaders stated they would follow their gut,
although they included gathering data important to their overall
decision making. What we learn from them is that they primarily
listen to themselves while seeking data. They have a deep trust for
themselves. How is this type of trust developed? In the field of
psychology, Carl Rogers founded an approach called the
"Humanistic approach." His premise was that it was imperative for
people to develop a positive self-regard. He wasn't speaking of only
following your gut but through self-improvement, you build a
stronger foundation and a basis for trusting your instincts and
judgement, as well as promoting loving yourself instead of being
controlled by others. Begin by really listening to what you say to
yourself, closely examining how you approach completing your own
ideas. The next thing is to set goals! We all love extreme goals,
reaching for all the gusto you can get, but not obtaining these goals
and failing causes greater harm to your self-esteem and your quest
to build self-trust. I would advise you to break that huge goal into
bite-size pieces, something you can achieve easily moving you
toward the big deal. With each conquest, you will build greater trust
for yourself. You have heard many times to improve your
weaknesses! I want to encourage you in the opposite direction.
Instead of trying to improve what you may be weak in, begin
building your strengths, using them for your God, your position,
your family, and the world. If you are not sure what your strengths
are, ask people you have faith in, people you know love you. Accept
your strengths by beginning to invest time and effort improving
them. Finally, be true to yourself; don't be afraid for people to see

the real you. It takes real strength to be vulnerable; it's not a weakness. When you live being afraid of people seeing the real you, what you are saying is you are not good enough. What happens is, you come across as being phony and dishonest and you get the opposite of what you need.

> *"Vulnerability sounds like truth and feels like courage. Truth and courage aren't always comfortable, but they're never weakness."*
> **— Brené Brown**

The greatest lesson we can all learn is that if we seek to be trustworthy, we must first trust ourselves.

Being vulnerable, or simply talking about vulnerability, is very difficult for me. Because early in my childhood I was raised in a very poor environment where those who were vulnerable were considered weak, and therefore open to the predators of the area. Building strength for the children living there meant putting on a false face and not showing yourself vulnerable to anything or anyone. I learned as I grew older, and especially when my family moved out of that area, that those learned traits had me closed off to important relationships. This was because my learned responses were to puff up and act confident when I needed and desired the help from the people around me. My inward thoughts were that they wouldn't like me if I was vulnerable, and worse, they may take advantage of me. Pushing myself to a positive mindset perspective has caused me to take risks. That risk is called vulnerability. I believe we can learn new skills and talents once we come to grips with being vulnerable to the right people. Looking deep into vulnerability reveals that it is not the act of being weak or submissive to everyone, as I thought; it is the courage to be yourself. Real vulnerability involves uncertainty, risk, and emotional exposure. It's just natural for us to guard our deepest desires and avoid having them trampled upon, rejected or left unfulfilled. Please don't think I am saying this is an easy process, especially if you have tried being vulnerable and you had your desires trampled on, rejected and unfulfilled. Often, because of past hurts, wounds, and injuries, you have avoided the process of becoming self-aware and gaining needed communication skills to unlock the loving, authentic and mutually supportive relationship you yearn for. Most of us hold a laundry list of reasons we aren't open to people and that list can include rejection, attack, lack of reciprocity, betrayal, or the loss of our own autonomy, just to mention the top five on our list. But if we are to reap the benefits of lifelong meaningful relationships, vulnerability is required. The inability to be vulnerable is influenced by those early relationships. If your early relationships were stable and loving you tend to have an easier time opening yourself to others. But if you were deprived of attention or were given mixed messages about your value and worth, or worse you were abandoned as a child, these experiences can cause you to expect the same treatment from everyone you encounter. It is through these experiences that every encounter in our lives are framed. These past experiences become the measuring rod we use to determine if our shield of rejection remains on high alert or not! If people get too close or they are too loving, your subconscious sends warnings to your mind flashing memories of your past hurts, hindering you from fully enjoying a new friend or romantic interest, and therefore hindering you from receiving the benefits of these relationships. Reactions can range from killing a relationship due to the smallest conflict or clinging to relationships even though they have become harmful to you. You may ask what can be done to begin to embrace the skill of vulnerability. Remember, the journey to change always begins on the inside before it is evident on the outside. Pay attention to your feelings over the next 24-hour period. Keep a record of your emotions throughout this time period. Record how you reacted to these emotions; what did you do? Or what should you have done about these emotions? When you take time to become more aware of your emotions, thoughts and feelings help you see what's wrong and what you need to change in order to feel better. Be sure to make note of any self-destructive acts; this will help you determine what's not where you would like it to be.

Once you have the recorded information, speak with someone you trust or your mentor about it. Talking to a loved one can bring you closer and talking to a mentor will assist you with moving forward. It doesn't matter how sound your mind may be; the belief we hold from past experiences form our present reality. These beliefs tend to cloud how we receive and interpret the behavior of others we are connected to. By speaking with a trusted friend, loved one or mentor, you won't fall into the old habit of dismissing your feelings or qualifying them based on past issues. The conversation should help you determine if your feelings are in line with the facts of your situation. Vulnerability is truly the key to lasting relationships. C.S. Lewis said, *"To love at all is to be vulnerable."* Loving means dropping your guard and allowing people in to see the real you. It means daring to show the authentic you! Yes! The 'YOU' that you're not altogether happy with. The one that disagrees with how you look, how tall you are, how short you are, the color of your hair, or skin and all the other things in you that haven't been resolved! Embrace the magnificent person and personality that God has created you to be and to become. Being authentic is an ever-evolving growth pattern. What you embrace is who you are today while remaining open to who you're going to be when God gets through with you! What an awesome thought and dream of envisioning that God is working everything in your life, the good things, the bad things, the hurtful things, everything stirred together for your good and to bring you to His prepared destiny for your life. Wow, what a beautiful picture of the you God has called and anointed you to become! So, to begin practicing vulnerability allow yourself to feel a deeper place of honesty with yourself and others, not the place that this generation calls just being 100%, which they believe gives them license to be rude! But this honesty begins with telling yourself the truth and embracing a God-envisioned truth about you. His truth is that you are a Designer's original with all your issues and problems. You were fearfully and wonderfully made. (Psalm 139:14) Walking in that truth empowers you to live freely in your newly-found vulnerability and enables you to be transparent not only with your truth but also when you are wrong. You can easily accept and admit when you are the one who has made the mistake, instead of being defensive and attacking those who bring it to your attention. Vulnerability will help you hear and accept what's being said as well as share your feelings about the situation willfully. Having the ability to accept your failures without being defensive is the next step toward living out this fundamental skill. You will notice that practicing the above skills gives you the needed courage to be okay with the times when things don't go quite right for you, and also gives you the patience and grace to gain a higher level of understanding the failures, and when others let you down. It is amazing how letting your guard down and allowing people and problems in gives you deeper, more loving relationships with friends, family, and lovers. This change pulls the dark curtains off the windows of the lonely and isolated corners of your mind. As you change, the Bible calls us to practice gratitude in good times and bad times. It says teach us, You should, with joy and thanksgiving, make your requests to God. (Philippians 4:6) So regardless of what may be occurring in your life at this moment, be sure to share it with God because only He can work it for your good. Begin believing that you are good enough and more than enough for everyone!

> Lord, "Give me insight so I can do what you tell me ... My whole life one long obedient response."
> — *(Psalms 119:34, MSG)*

I understand that this is no overnight endeavor. It absolutely will take time and you will have to be intentional in putting these principles into practice. I believe that if you truly desire to make significant changes in your life so that it affects everyone and everything you put your hand to, you will make the commitment to work on becoming the best *you* ever! Take baby steps to begin with; accomplish one goal at a time. After you have completed that first step, you will gain the balance you need to make the next step. Before long, you will be leaping through these skills until they become a vital part of all your relationships. As you take on this risky change, be prepared to be misunderstood by others. Others may become angry because they want you to remain the same. The issue for them is if you change, they must change, too. Some will label you, or worse reject you and call your changes fake. Fighting these issues can be daunting, especially coming against the fear of rejection. Remember, being held to that place is not where you want to be. You are moving to the place of true authenticity which means practicing vulnerability. The gain is so much greater than the pain if you continue your growth in this area.

In a world where everything and everyone is applying pressure on your emotions and mind, their purpose is to cause you to conform to their ideas of what behaviors are acceptable or unacceptable. The world loves conformity, but you have been called to true authenticity being true and honest to yourself and therefore to others. It is living in a way that your words align with your behavior. You are known to others as a person who doesn't pretend, act fake, or is two-faced. The ability to live in the presence of who you are really drives you to knowing your inner beliefs, knowing what you value and living from that place in all you say and do. This means you are willing to evaluate every relationship, including jobs and personal relationships to ensure they do not infringe on the authentic you or violate your truth about you. If you are in that type of situation, you must be willing to leave or walk away from that relationship or job that violates your personal code. To begin this higher level of living, you must practice listening to your spirit which speaks wisdom to you, assisting you so your life has less drama and strife. Your life is yours to design the journey God has established for you. Striving for excellence begins in you. It is the world that's readily available to you; it is also the one you have or can acquire the power to change. This is intentional living! Being authentic or genuine has its limitations. These limits are based on your circumstances or the "circle where you stand." Your ability to develop the authentic you will be influenced by these circumstances which include social, religious, cultural, family, political and other characteristics. To become intentional in this process means you keep your focus on who you want to be or become, rather than what you're fighting through.

CHAPTER SIX

BEHAVIOR

Acting Out Is Not an Act at All!

"A person without self-control is like a city with broken-down walls".
— **(Proverbs 25:28, New Living Translation, NLT)**

"You can't talk your way out of a problem you behaved yourself into."
— **Stephen M. R. Covey**

———————— ༄༅ ————————

I have been taught that self-control is the ability to control impulses and reactions; it is another name for self-discipline. My parents were big on discipline. They believed and taught their eight children that if you cannot control yourself you cannot control anything. Having well-mannered and controlled children was my mother's life goal. She completed this task with grace and strength, being one of very few women in our church who could bring her children to any program or meeting, who knew how to be respectful, quiet and under control. As I got older and mature, I learned this skill was rare among my friends who were known to exercise little to no degrees of self-control.

I had a friend in college, her name was Linda. Linda seemed quiet, demure and in full control of herself, always, until one afternoon when we decided to go to the mall together to shop, and Linda drove. It was a nice, warm Saturday afternoon and we were feeling happy and joyful to take time away from our studies. As we approached a popular California mall, the freeway became extremely congested with drivers jockeying in and out of lanes trying to gain a better vantage point. As other drivers cut into our lane causing Linda to slam on the brakes, she became noticeably angry and irritated. Before long, her irritation grew. It was unchecked by skills of self-control, to the degree that my nice quiet, demure Linda was cutting into other lanes, yelling out the window choice profanity, and giving any onlooker the finger. I was at first intrigued by her behavior, and quietly watched as I told myself, "Boy, did I have her wrong!" When we finally arrived, by the grace of God, she noticed I was quiet and asked, "What's up?" I said, "Nothing, really, but I would have never thought you would lose it!" Linda began to justify her reaction as being caused by the other drivers. I didn't object, but I began to recall my mother teaching her children, "A person who can control themselves is greater than a general who overthrows a city!" Wow, 'greater than!' It set me in motion to monitor my own actions so that others didn't have to do it for me. Self-discipline is one of the most important tools for self-improvement and a catalyst for achieving personal success.

It is the ingredient in gold that makes it valuable. Self-discipline is vital for overcoming obsessions, fears, addictions, and any unwanted behavior. It provides the strength to master your moods. Your successes will be measured by you doing the right thing, even when you aren't in the mood to do it. When you have learned self-discipline, you also control what you say. The Scripture says, *"Be careful what you say and protect your life. A careless talker destroys himself."* (Proverbs 13:3, *GNT*). People who have learned the self-discipline of self-control watch their words because the power of life and death is in the tongue. But when you have disciplined yourself with self-control, other people can't cause you to act one way or another. Your behavior is under your control and you will never give that control to anyone but God Himself. Part of learning the skill of self-discipline is knowing your limits, what you can and cannot take, how quickly you become angry and what you do with that emotion. Are you always slightly hot-tempered? Then the cooling agent of self-discipline must be practiced bringing your emotions under control. The Bible teaches, *"If you are sensible, you will control your temper. When someone wrongs you, it is a great virtue to ignore it."* (Proverbs 19:11, *GNT*) Learning to discipline yourself has it benefits:

- *It keeps self-destructive behaviors in check (addictions, obsessions, and compulsive behaviors).*
- *It enables you to master and have balance over your life.*
- *It eliminates the feeling of helplessness and the debilitating trait of over-dependence on others.*
- *It helps keep your emotional responses in check or at least within boundaries.*
- *It helps you maintain mental and emotional detachment enabling peace of mind.*

- *It makes you a responsible person worthy of trust*
- *It allows you to detect destructive moods, rejecting them and other negative feelings and thoughts.*
- *It gives you permission to take charge of your life.*
- *It builds and strengthens self-esteem, confidence, inner strength, self-mastery, and willpower.*

These are just to name a few of the benefits of practicing the discipline of self-control. All of these are desirable of everyone seeking to find success for their lives. When you have failed to practice the discipline of self-control, your entire life is off balance. Your schedules are off either by over-volunteering or always being late. Your team either expects you to be late or they tell you an earlier meeting time because of your lack of self-discipline. If you don't control how you allot your time, everyone else will control it for you. When you don't value your time and talents, no one else will either. They will treat you as disposable, and your time as being always available, because you have not established a discipline of controlling yourself and your time. Do you often feel like there isn't enough hours in the day? Does it always look like others accomplish more than you in the same amount of time? Do you feel like you're always behind the eight ball? Do you deal with the constant uneasiness of not sure you're prepared? Because you put the project together over the last few hours, you tell yourself you're too busy but you're creative enough to do it in the last minute! Have you ever asked others how they perceive your performance? The Bible indicates, *"Don't waste your time on useless work, mere busywork, the barren pursuits of darkness. Expose these things for the sham they are.*

It's a scandal when people waste their lives on things they must do in the darkness where no one will see. Rip the cover off those frauds and see how attractive they look in the light of Christ.

> Wake up from your sleep,
> Climb out of your coffins;
> Christ will show you the light!

So, watch your step. Use your head. Make the most of every chance you get. These are desperate times! (Ephesians 5:11-16, MSG)

Practicing the discipline of self-control enables you to manage your money to move you toward success. You learn to live on less than you make and invest the difference. It will teach you the value of a budget which tells your money where you want it to go, rather than wondering where it went and on what it was spent. People who practice this discipline don't wonder or worry about their money because they control its flow instead of being controlled by it. "In the house of the wise are stores of choice food and oil, but a foolish man devours all he has." (Proverbs 21:20, NIV) Once you have learned self-discipline, everything in your life comes in line and under your control. This theory holds true for every area, including your body because people with self-control maintain their health, so that they can accomplish more and enjoy their achievements. The Bibles says in 1 Thessalonians 4:4 (MSG) "Learn to appreciate and give dignity to your body … " From the discussion above, it should confront you with the need for determining which areas in your life you lack the discipline of self-control. The disciplines you establish today will determine your future success.

But it takes more than just willpower for lasting self-control. It takes a power greater than yourself: "For the Spirit that God has given us does not make us timid; instead, his Spirit fills us with power, love, and self-control." (2 Timothy 1:7, GNT)

The Power to Control Yourself

The very thought of trying to control yourself leads us to understand that the fight is on! For Christians, it is not unlike what the children of Israel encountered in trying to possess the Promised Land that God was giving them. It was promised to them, but they had to take it by force, one town at a time. In the same way they fought for what was rightfully theirs, we too must fight for our promised gift of self-control and take it by force.

Self-control is a battle between a divided self! There is a quote I remember hearing that says:

> *"Two natures beat within my breast*
> *The one is foul, the one is blessed*
> *The one I love, the one I hate.*
> *The one I feed will dominate."*
> **— Anonymous**

It tells us that our 'self' produces thoughts and desires we should not satisfy; they push us further to resist and not control it. The Scripture teaches us to "deny ourselves" and "take up our cross daily." (Luke 9:23) We are to exercise self-control like athletes, but our goal is not temporary like ribbons and medals; it is eternal. Athletes push themselves and force their bodies to obey their demands to become winners. They must continue this discipline even when they don't feel like it. Self-control is saying no to sinful desires, even when it hurts. A Christians level of self-control is not a "just say no" campaign set in motion by some politician or a well-meaning group. Your "No" is rooted by faith in the immeasurable power and pleasure of Jesus Christ. In this way, our "No" gives Christ all the glory.

The foundational strength of the Christian view of self-control is that it is a gift from God. According to Galatians 5:22, 23, we have been given character gifts from God through the Holy Spirit. These gifts are called "The fruit of the Spirit" and they are, love, joy, peace, patience, kindness, goodness, faithfulness, gentleness, and self-control. Even the best of us struggle and fight to control ourselves and it is a great fight when you're trying to do it in your own strength. Zechariah 4:6 should be our daily mantra, *"Not by might nor by power, but by My Spirit, says the Lord of hosts."* You shouldn't feel bad that there are times you seem to lose the fight because you're fighting in your own strength. If you win by your own strength and might, then you get the glory. But when you step out in faith by the Lord's Spirit, then God gets the glory and you get the victory over this battle. So how do we utilize this fruit gift? Glad you asked. We accomplish this by staying in God's Word (the Bible), and by receiving His grace which enables us to trust all that God is for us in Jesus. This grace that God gives us helps us to deny worldly desires in this present age according to Titus 2:11, 12. When you receive this grace deep inside, you are given the power to break wrong desires and behavior. The fight for self-control, ultimately, is a faith fight. You are empowered to fight the good fight of faith so that you have the strength to take hold of the eternal life that God has lovingly given to you.

I would say most of us were dealing with anger at least once this past week. It may have been a minor infraction of being cut off on the highway, long lines at the grocery store or the irritation of getting the kids to clean their rooms. More often, it's a situation at work or an unresolved issue at home with your spouse or loved one. Many adults carry childhood hurts that rise to the surface at the most unexpected times. Our society is full of angry people who cannot or will not deal with the ugly monster that rises from the background of our minds at will. Okay, I know you're thinking, "THAT, is not me! I'm Christ-like and I always ask, 'What would Jesus do?'" Well, the first step to any recovery or deliverance is to admit that you, too, struggle with anger. You may be one of those closet angry folks who acts out in passive-aggressive ways. So, when you see others waving their hands, with elevated voices, red faces, and extended neck veins, you immediately think, 'I would never!' *The Christian Counselor's Manual),* by Jay E. Adams states, "Anger is a problem for every Christian; sinful anger is probably involved in 90 percent of all counseling problems." Can you imagine what would happen in our world if everyone took the time to deal with their anger? Many number one killing health problems would clear up. Murder, child abuse, divorce, and terrorism, as well as the wars they incite would stop.

Many leading doctors have attributed anger to heart and cardiovascular disease. Anger could also be a byproduct of overeating and excess weight gain, leading to obesity. This is what the Bible says about this issue:

> *"But now you also, put them all aside: anger, wrath, malice, slander, and abusive speech from your mouth."*
> — *(Colossians 3:8, New American Standard Bible, NASB)*

The bigger question here is how do we put aside these negative behaviors and actions? It is amazing that the writer, Paul, was speaking to pagan people who had suffered great abuse by being involved in sinful pagan acts. No doubt these rituals must have left them scarred and full of anger. He simply told them to "put it all aside," Wow. Let's dig deeper to pull out of the text what Paul wants us to live by. It is quite clear there were no self-help groups available to help these new Christians. There were no life groups, no Christian counselors to lead and guide them through a prescribed process. Except by faith, the expectation was that they had the power to control their own behavior and deal with what was controlling them. The Bible gives clear guidelines for being angry. Ephesians 4:26 tells us, *"Be angry, and yet do not sin; do not let the sun go down on your anger."* Then Paul tells us to put aside all anger. Scripture seems to indicate that anger has dimensions, and it can either be righteous or sinful. Let's dig at the root of this emotion and find out how we can tell the difference. Taking the time to analyze your own anger and depth of where is arises from will assist you with knowing if your stance is righteous, sinful, or mixed. You can't make wise moves unless you know the ground you're standing on.

The Bible is clear on its teaching of anger. It tells us that righteous anger is the godly reaction to sin or injustice, and the wrath of God is His settled opposition against sin. Most biblical references to anger are about God's anger, not human anger. The Bible tells us that Jesus became angry when He encountered unbelief and hypocrisy. Our desire is to be like Him; the object of our anger should be the ungodly acts and not the person committing them. So, your starting point in determining which type of anger you harbor is to stop and take an honest analysis. Ask yourself, 'Was I feeling righteous anger about that upsetting issue, sinful anger, or a mixture of both?' While you're analyzing, think about why you're angry. Remember, God Himself, used this approach in Genesis 4:6 with Cain when He asked, "Why are you angry?" God never asks questions to gain information. He's God; He already knows. But He asks to help us think about the situation from His perspective. Cain justifies his anger and jealousy with his brother Abel

because God accepted his brother's sacrifice and not his. God encourages Cain to do what's right, despite his anger and jealousy with his brother. God also warned Cain that when we are entertaining anger, sin is right at the door, ready to consume us. Many of us ignore God's warning about this destructive emotion. In the end of the story, Cain kills his brother.

It is so easy to justify sinful anger by claiming that it is righteous, meaning you have a right to be that angry and you have a right to be angry with that person. By telling yourself the truth through analyzing where the anger is coming from, you will realize that even our righteous anger is tainted by sinful anger. That is because most of our anger is rooted in selfishness. When you open your anger before God and find that there is selfishness, you must realize it is sinful. As you read through these instructions you may be thinking, 'How is this helping me? If I admit my anger to God and find that it is sinful, that will do nothing but make me feel guilty!' On the contrary, the Bible is filled with solutions for sin to give you victory over your life. With the Word of God, you are not out of control and the best news is that you can control your sinful anger. Our Lord and Savior died to take away the guilt of sin, and to give us power through the indwelling of the Holy Spirit to overcome our sins. Remember, the Bible never requires us to do what we cannot do without the power of God's Holy Spirit. It is God Who gives us the strength to obey His Word. God is absolutely concerned about the intent of our heart, so it is imperative that we don't live in anger all week and show up to worship service on Sunday. You may fool other worshippers at church, but God is never fooled. Most folks get bundled into knots when they pretend they are not angry. But the Bible teaches that anger must be expressed in positive ways by doing what's right and acceptable in the sight of God. He teaches us how to express that anger in ways that could save a relationship or bring peace to an otherwise destructive and potentially volatile situation. One difference between our anger and God's anger is that, since we aren't always holy and pure, we often get angry at things that aren't true wrongs, or at things that don't really matter to anyone but us. God is angry with things that are not righteous, true, pure, edifying, or holy. God is always calling us to act and react with Jesus in mind, "What would Jesus do?" because godly anger constructively engages what is wrong in a way that is patient, merciful, forgiving, and honest in tackling what needs tackling. Our sinful anger causes hurt, destruction, and alienation. Godly anger becomes an instrument in God's hands to make this bad world better. As you work toward who God has called you to be, practicing what Jesus did ensures that we are our best selves.

It seems difficult to almost impossible to find people who live with integrity, not just practicing it as an art but living it as a lifestyle. Every person should seek a life full of integrity. This character trait is not just doing what you believe; it is allowing the mind of Christ to direct your behavior and actions. For you to become a person that impacts your friends, family, and significant others in a positive and powerful way, you must include this character into your personal "must haves!" If you took the time to speak with people about integrity, they most likely would say, "You're outdated in your thoughts and no one lives like that anymore." These days integrity is relative to what each person thinks is best for them!" But they are so wrong. Just as every healthy relationship needs trust, integrity is needed to sustain that trust. There is an

adage of, "If you can't trust someone in all areas, you can't trust them at all." Our character of integrity is compromised whenever we betray the smallest trust. No one can claim to be credible without integrity. What is integrity or trustworthiness? Glad you asked. Integrity is living with a strict adherence to a moral code, which is reflected in transparent honesty and complete harmony in what one thinks, says, and does. In application, it means to seek to know what's important to God and live in the light of that revelation. Integrity is acting based on subscribing to God's values as listed and described in His Word, (the Bible). By the leading of the Holy Spirit, we conform and develop a lifestyle of conduct according to those values. Integrity begins as the foundation of every life and it grows to be the nails in a sure place. These nails of integrity are holding the entire building together despite being under the intense pressures of life. For Christians, integrity is the basic characteristic that God looks for in those He brings closer. You cannot gain integrity like you would a reputation or applause from others. Integrity is a trait of the heart; it is the character trait of a morally and spiritually healthy person, and of course one that effective leaders have.

It is important that this crucial trait not be confused with reputation. I was invited to participate in a production in CA. I was asked to be the emcee for a program with award-winning singers and artists. The producer had a great reputation of putting on shows that were packed out and I was flattered to be asked. I was told to just get there, and they would reimburse my travel expenses and pay for my services. Due to the company's reputation I agreed. After I arrived, I quickly learned that all the promises were lies. The artists were very angry for lack of payment and unfulfilled contract agreements. The producer wrote me a check (which bounced a couple of times) and left me feeling used and disillusioned. That company's reputation had hit the floor for me. I wondered how the packed-out crowd would view them, not to mention the singers and musicians. Their reputation could have been intact if they had integrity. Healthy strong and sound reputations are built from a foundation of integrity. Being young in my actions, I did not know that integrity can be traced by consistency. This consistency is not just seen by soft values like inner values and attitudes, but also by observable hard values like words and actions. It's clear the more consistent we are, the higher degree of integrity we possess and the greater authentic reputation we receive. The Bible gives great examples of men and women who conducted their lives with integrity and received a great reputation. One example is Daniel. He was an upright man and God used him mightily. Daniel held his values and integrity in the face of slavery and hardship. Because he was consistent in his values, his integrity was known by the king and sought after to answer his dreams. Daniel was able to stand before the king without wavering and speak the truth of God due to his reputation as listed in Scripture.

> *"I have heard of you that the Spirit of God is in you, and that light and understanding and excellent wisdom are found in you.*
> *— (Daniel 5:14, NKJV).*

The king stated what he had heard of Daniel due to his integrity and reputation of consistency. These words went before Daniel. When people spoke of him, they listed his known behavior. We, too, are known by our behavior. Whether it's good or bad, in the end we will be known by our behavior, too. Integrity is a quality that's greater than gold; it is the basis of all trust. Integrity is the root of the tree that determines not only the fruit but the sweetness of the fruit. This level of integrity will either cause people to be drawn to the tree or they shun the tree. The way we live our lives speaks volumes of what we stand for. Conversely, it also yells that we stand for nothing. When your God-given belief system becomes your foundation, people believe you to be strong, solid and a dependable person, a person they can depend on being the same in all situations, which brings positive results to you enabling others to have confidence in you. The character trait of integrity brings with it the complimentary trait of humility. Humility supports a person of integrity by causing them to want to do more of what is right, rather than being seen more as always right! A humble person is concerned with perception; their intent is that how people perceive them is aligned with their belief system. So, these types of people put lots of effort into acting on good ideas rather than having good ideas. You will find these folks seeking new levels of truth rather than holding on to their positions. They work for the good of the team instead of trying to elevate themselves. They are all about recognizing the contributions of the team even if they are the contributor; they have no interest in self-elevation. Don't get me wrong, this level of humility or meekness is not weakness; to the contrary, it is power under control! Humble people recognize that they can accomplish so much more with complimentary people, not just anyone, because some people pull you away from your God-designed destiny. So humbly choosing your team as a compliment to each other working in harmony like a fine-tuned engine is part of what a person of integrity does well. The opposing traits to humility are arrogance and pride. These traits usually put personal ego, self-gain, and self-promotion above principles, and above others. This level of humility-infused integrity takes courage because it is so much easier to give into the pressures of our world than it is to stand. Often taking a stand for principles and values means you stand alone. All of us need models who have lived their lives exhibiting this type of integrity and courage. I want to present to you a great woman whose life is one all of us can use as a great example of integrity and humility. That woman is Queen Esther. Her story is found in the Old Testament in Esther 1-5. The story of Queen Esther is a dramatic, inspiring, and in some ways shocking story of the strength of a young woman. Esther was brought into the king's house to be in a lineup of young women to possibly be chosen as the next queen. The events recorded in the book of Esther reads like a newspaper account of our day and time. The Bible reports that Esther lived during a time of great oppression and racial discrimination against her people, the Jews. She lived with her uncle, Mordecai and his family in the city of Persia because Esther's parents died when she was very young. Esther was a victim of circumstance. Her uncle, Mordecai was warned by the prophet years earlier that God said they needed to flee Persia and return to their homeland to rebuild the temple. Mordecai, along with many other Jews, decided to ignore the directions of God and stay in Persia. They became comfortable in a foreign land, a place that did not accept them. Mordecai told Esther not to tell she was a Jew. The story lets us know that Esther kept her family secrets. It is also clear that God was working during these circumstances, orchestrating the events in Esther's life. God will do what He wills to carry out His plan and to keep His promises to those He loves. You must know that no matter where life leads you, God is always with you working life's circumstances for your good.

Esther was chosen, along with other young women her age, to live in the palace to possibly become the next queen. Mordecai worked for the king at the palace; he was a keeper at the gate controlling who could come into the palace. One day, as Mordecai was working at the gate, he overheard two of the king's men plotting. God had placed Mordecai in the right place at the right time. These two men were angry with King Xerxes, and they were making plans to kill him. Fortunately, Mordechai overheard them and told Esther, and she reported to the king that Mordecai had uncovered the plans against him. Esther's report to the king was checked out and it was found to be true. In turn, the king had his two officials put to death. By reporting this plot to the king, Esther and Mordecai saved the king's life. You would think this action would put them in good standing with the king and his court. However, the king had another official named Haman, whose family had a history of hating the Jews. They were prejudiced against them and went out of their way to destroy the Jews. Just like us, when you think all is well and everything is going to be great, the enemy has another agent to work against the people and the plan of God. Haman was promoted to a very high position by the king. The king even ordered everyone to bow down to Haman whenever they came in his presence. Mordecai held fast to his belief that he would not bow down to anyone except his God. He made this decision knowing who Haman was and how he felt about the Jews. When Haman came through the gate to get to the palace, Mordecai would not bow down. The king's officials asked him why he would not bow down as the king ordered when Haman came by. He told them it was because he was a Jew and he believed in the only living God, Jehovah. Mordecai's resistance to bow down was noticed by Haman, which made him furious. He also learned that Mordecai was a Jew, so out of anger, Haman came up with a plan not just to kill Mordecai but to kill all the Jews. This decision would get back at Mordecai as well as get rid of the race of people he had hated all his life. This would be no small feat; King Xerxes' kingdom was huge and far-reaching. It included many countries in which multiple hundreds of Jewish families were scattered. Haman took his plot to the king and the king trusted Haman so much he didn't seek counsel from his wise men as he had in the past. King Xerxes blindly followed Haman's dastardly plan of genocide of the

Jewish race. Haman involved the entire government in his plot to eradicate all Jews. He devised a plan to kill all Jews across the countryside on the same day. The king gave Haman his ring with the royal seal. Once the letter with the orders was written and marked with the royal seal, this could not be stopped. After helping Esther and Mordecai get in good standing with the king, would he allow this evil official to complete his plan in destroying the Jewish race? Well, the Jews who stayed in Persia were in direct opposition and disobedient to God's instructions. If Mordecai and the other Jews had obeyed God, there would not have been any Jews in Persia for Haman to kill. We must understand that when we follow God's directions, it places us within His hand of protection. When we disobey, we must struggle to seek God's intervention in the consequences of our disobedience. It's no wonder that all the Jews in Persia were in mourning because the day of their death was quickly approaching. Mordecai again sent word to Esther, as well as a copy of the letter decreeing all Jews would die on that day. Mordecai told Esther she had to go and plead for the lives of her people. Esther was terrified and hesitant to go before the king, not only did he not know she was a Jew herself, there were very strict laws about visiting the king. No one could just come into the palace to talk with the king. If he hadn't sent for them, they would have to wait until he pointed his royal scepter at them for them to speak to him. This rule was especially enforced for women. Esther sent this information to Mordecai so that he would know it was not easy for her to take on the task he was requesting of her. Mordecai replied reminding Esther that she too was a Jew, and it would not be long after killing all the other Jews that her life would be in danger, too.

Besides, she lives in the palace and could only hide for a short time. He also told her that if she refused to help her people, help would come from another place because the God that promised to make them great was faithful. Esther considered Mordecai's request and accepted the challenge gathering all the courage she could under the circumstances. She even told Mordecai to ask the Jews to fast for three days on her behalf; after that, she would go before King Xerxes without being summoned. After the fast, three days later, Esther got all dressed up in her finest royal robes mustering all the courage within her as she approached the king's court. Can you imagine the fear running down her spine, the nervousness in her heart as she walked toward the throne room? I can imagine her in a cold sweat, hands shaking, knees knocking as she moved toward what could be certain death for her. If King Xerxes does not point his royal scepter at her, she would be put to an immediate death, which ultimately means all the Jews in the kingdom would die, too. I am sure her mind was racing as she thought about the pressure of thousands of people resting on her shoulders, not to mention her own life. But against all odds, Esther sent a note to her uncle Mordecai saying, *"(After this fast), will I go in unto the king, which is not according to the law: and if I perish, I perish."* (Esther 4:16) She must have been thinking it's a just thing to break an unjust law! There she stood, in clear view of the king! 'Oh, God, what am I doing? Oh, God, I'm so scared!' This had to be the dictates of her heart. Esther was stepping out with the strength of integrity, strength we call courage that literally takes every fiber of your being. It is self-denial and self-sacrificing; it stretches your soul causing you to feel like you can soar, a level of courage that's God-infused, a power that's bigger than all outdoors. As God orchestrated her steps, the king saw her and motioned for Esther to come forward. 'It's actually happening; he didn't call the guards to drag me out and kill me!' The King interrupted her thoughts of triumph. He asked, *"What wilt thou, queen Esther? and what is thy request? it shall be even given thee to the half of the kingdom."* (Esther 5:3) God had given her so much favor that the king said that whatever she asked, he would give up to half his kingdom! Wow! But Esther had to play it cool! She had to be wise, so she invited the king and his official Haman to have dinner with her and they agreed. Haman was so excited to be asked to dinner by the queen that he bragged to his wife and friends about this special attention, and that she invited him to a second dinner date along with the king. Haman was an evil man and full of pride; the attention of the queen did not change his plot. Haman was still angry with Mordecai and he still wanted all the Jews killed. Haman's wife Zeresh suggested he build a special gallows to hang Mordecai, to help relieve some of Haman's anger, and he did just that. In the meantime, the king was having trouble sleeping so he asked a servant to come and bring him the book of records of the chronicles. While reading over the activities of his kingdom for the previous week, he noticed that Mordecai was the one who exposed the plot to kill him and therefore saved his life. The king noticed that Mordecai had not been rewarded for stopping the plot against him, so he determined in his mind to reward Mordecai in some way.

It is amazing how God works in the middle of a mess. When things seem totally out of control, don't ever think all is lost; even to the very end God is always in control. Just as the king was pondering what to do for Mordecai, Haman entered the court. Haman was on a mission to get permission to hang Mordecai in his newly-built gallows. But before Haman could make his request, the king asked Haman what he should do to honor the man who saved his life, to show him the king's favor. Haman, thinking the king was talking about him, began to describe this lavish plan for the king to honor the man he believed to be himself.

> **This is what Haman said:**
>
> "Have your servants get a royal robe you have worn. Have them bring a horse you have ridden on. Have a royal mark placed on its head. Then give the robe and horse to one of your most noble princes. Let the robe be put on the man you want to honor. Let him be led on the horse through the city streets. Let people announce in front of him, 'This is what is done for the man the king wants to honor!'"
> — (Esther 6:8, 9, New International Reader's Version, NIRV)

Haman was celebrating internally with his idea. He must have thought, 'This is going to be great! I can just picture me in this grand parade through the streets of the kingdom, sitting high on the king's royal horse!' While he was in the midst of his daydreaming, the king interrupted his vision in all its glamour by saying, "Go right away, … get the robe. Bring the horse. Do exactly what you have suggested. Do it for Mordecai, the Jew." (Esther 6:10, NIRV) The king said it was because Mordecai saved his life! That statement was a blow to Haman's ego and pride! It took the wind right out of his sails. It infuriated him to the max, but Haman did just what the king said and honored Mordecai in the way he described to the king. Afterward, Haman returned home, ashamed, and embarrassed. He tried to lift his spirits by preparing for the second banquet with Queen Esther. Finally, Esther, Haman, and the king were seated and ready for the highly anticipated banquet, as well as the anticipated request from the queen. The Bible indicates that Queen Esther finally answers the king this way:

> *"Then Queen Esther answered, 'King Xerxes, I hope you will show me your favor. I hope you will be pleased to let me live. That's what I want. Please spare my people. That's my appeal to you. My people and I have been sold to be destroyed. We've been sold to be killed and wiped out."*
> *— (Esther 7:3, 4, NIRV)*

There, it was out there; Esther finally said it! She asked the king to spare her life and the lives of her people. Don't forget, the king did not know Esther was a Jew. At first, the king did not realize who Esther was talking about, this person that wanted to kill all the Jews. The king demanded, *"Who is the man who has dared to do such a thing? And where is he?"* Esther decided to tell the king everything. She said, *"The man hates us! He's our enemy! He's this evil Haman!"* In the end, the king decided Haman would take Mordecai's place on the gallows he himself had built. (Esther 7:5-9, *NIRV*) Esther's courage was evident throughout the story. There may be things in your life that are difficult, something that causes you fear. It may be something that you must take a stand for, using all the courage you can to overcome the issue. Sometimes the issues are because we've made bad choices. But there are times in our lives that we have not done anything to cause the circumstances we're struggling with. We must know in our hearts that we never stand alone, and that God is sovereign in all things and our courage comes from Him alone. Our God is bigger than our circumstances, greater than our troubles, stronger than our weakest moments and bigger than the biggest person in your life. He told us in His Word that He would work

142

everything together for our good. This doesn't mean we can just live recklessly and do whatever we want thinking God will pick up all our troubles and make them right. The Bible is clear that we cannot test or challenge God in this way. We are admonished to follow God's instructions, which in turn allows us to enjoy the very best that God has for us. The greatest courage we can show is conquering the issues of our own lives.

Standing up to fear and the desire to quit. Having the strength to stare failure in the eye and say I will try again! Courage is a character trait of integrity that must be learned and practiced daily.

> *"Courage is rightly esteemed the first of human qualities because it is the quality which guarantees all others."*
> — *Winston Churchill*

People who live their lives with courage seem to have the dexterity to keep going despite the challenges life may bring them. It takes courage to believe that the best is yet to come, and you are better than you believe or can see today. Courage is such a powerful trait; it is a proven fact that when you exercise the tenacity to believe you will be alright, your percentage of being alright increases by 30 % over those who live in fear. Medically, it is proven that those patients who come with courage and a tenacity to get well, more often than not, get better. Courage is not the absence of fear, because courageous people are scared to the core of their beings. But they refuse to live their lives in fear, so they dig down deep and make themselves go forward. They refuse to allow their mind to say, "I can't do it" and lead from their heart which says, "I must do it!" This process begins with redefining who we are. We no longer define ourselves by our fears, "I'm so scared! You know I'm not strong" and the statement used by many, "I'm too shy!" No matter where these labels are birthed from, once they are conceived in your mind and heart and birthed in your life they begin to control your thoughts and then your life entirely. Many people think they are broken or that something is wrong with them. Because of this toxic thinking, they live their lives within the boundaries of these labels, afraid to venture out. Practicing this thinking keeps you living in a box, unable to move forward or move to a more satisfying and fulfilling way of life. Breaking out of this cycle takes more than just changing your address, moving to a new state, or changing your job, although these changes may be included along with the most important change of all. That important change is changing your mind! When you change your mind, everything else in your life will follow. It must be a hard change, something you intentionally do, something you have plans to do and that you have specified some life habits to incorporate as you move forward. You establish habits to walk out your life in courageous ways. This may be facing the thing that frightens you most! Even if you must face it daily until you stare it down, develop the habit of looking right at it. The more you do it or practice this habit, the easier it is to move forward. I do not want to suggest that this is easy to accomplish. Moving in courage for the first time can be tough and scary, like standing before a full auditorium of people to give your speech, or looking across the net at the tennis player you have never beaten, or applying for the job you qualify for but lack the confidence to believe it's yours! Any one of these could be reasons to send you running but fortify your thoughts by avoiding the temptation to overthink your decision. Or worse, talk yourself out of trying at all. If you find yourself moving backward in your decisions, start working out! Run, join a class, and get moving because building your body in turn builds your mind. Start small and gradually increase your physical strength to increase your mental strength.

CHAPTER SEVEN

THE MOST FASCINATING ME I'VE NEVER MET!

———— ୬୧୬ᕥ ————

Have you ever wondered what you would be if you didn't worry about failure? Have you ever looked at a faraway star and wondered how high or how far you could go if you loved yourself? The power you can receive by accepting who you are and your potential is limitless. This reality of acceptance has mysteries, levels, and avenues untraveled because most people will not begin with accepting who they are. Most of our time and energy is spent on trying to get other people to accept us. The Psalmist, David, when he finally realized who God had created him to be, wrote it this way:

"Oh yes, you shaped me first inside, then out; you formed me in my mother's womb. I thank you, High God—you're breathtaking! Body and soul, I am marvelously made! I worship in adoration—what a creation! You know me inside and out, you know every bone in my body;

You know exactly how I was made, bit by bit, how I was sculpted from nothing into something.

Like an open book, you watched me grow from conception to birth; all the stages of my life were spread out before you, The days of my life all prepared before I'd even lived one day." (Psalm139:13-16, MSG)

Wow! That Scripture right there ought to fill your eyes with tears and your heart with wonder at why a God so perfect and pure would create you with possibility and promise. It is a profound promise that if you can believe, you can become all that God designed you to be. Grabbing hold of the fascinating you can be as fleeting as trying to catch lightening bugs in a mason jar. I wasn't raised in the country, but I loved going to my Uncle John's farm in the summer. It seemed like the longest ride of my life, but once we arrived in Kansas City, Kansas, I waited in anticipation of chasing bugs who accented the night with their light. They were best seen in the country because there were no streetlights like in the city where I was raised. Some areas of the country had lots of trees causing the night to appear as dark as a hundred midnights. But these small insignificant bugs could light up a dark spot like nothing else could, creating a glow that made the night a fascinating mystery in the mind of a child. This is like what God has created on the inside of you, a fascinating light which you have yet to discover. Have you looked inward? Have you dug deep into the corners of your own soul? Isn't it strange how most of us waste years of life trying to become what others say we should be, instead of investing life in becoming the fascinating person we were created to be? You were designed with precision and care, with the loving touch of our Father, God. The intricacy of your internal design informs your external look. It's by far more than superficial features. Instead, it shines as bright as the lightening bugs secretly illuminating the purposeful destiny of your life. Time spent trying to live out someone else's destiny is like the biblical story of the child David, who went to the battlefield and was confronted by King Saul. The king wanted a warrior to go to battle and David volunteered, but King Saul felt David wouldn't be successful unless David wore the King's amour to go and fight the giant, Goliath. It may have been David's fight, but the amour wasn't designed for him!! He would have been walking in someone else's shoes or literately someone else's amour! David was a boy of great courage, but he could not fit the King's amour, which was designed for the King's stature, build and height. Like David, you and your life are unique and fascinating because you were designed to attract others to your light, and to hold their attention because you hope against hope. You have character and personal charm coupled with your unusual nature. When you embrace *you*, the person you haven't met yet, there is a special quality that fills your soul with vivacious passion. This passion tells the world that you are one of a kind, a Designer's original, just like Job said about the simple things in life like rain and snow.

Job said, *"God's voice thunders in marvelous ways; he does great things beyond our understanding. He says to the snow, 'Fall on the earth,' and to the rain shower, 'Be a mighty downpour.'"* (Job 37:5, 6, *NIV*). Even God commands the elements to be themselves and do what they were created to do!

He is doing the same thing with you, so you stop trying to make yourself into the person you wish to be long enough to hear His voice thunder an introduction of the person He has called you to be.

But you have not met yet. When a person has not come to know the gift and treasure they possess, they settle for less, less from people, less from life, and they begin to believe they don't deserve more or better. Many come to the misguided conclusion that whatever we can get is better than nothing. The problem with that mentality is that better than nothing is really nothing in disguise.

Whenever you gain something that is neither satisfying nor enjoyable, it is like having nothing at all. When you must talk yourself into being nice, kind or excited, instead of experiencing the love, joy, and passion of the thing, it's settling for less. When you think of a relationship, business, or venture, and you're only counting the time and energy you put into it, there is no love, gratification or joy; you have settled. When you spend more time complaining about the cost instead of enjoying the journey, you have settled indeed. If this describes you and your life,

you are learning what you believe about yourself and your value. It is time to dig deep until you find who God has created you to be.

> *"Friendship with oneself is all important, because without it one cannot be friends with anyone else in the world."*
> — *Eleanor Roosevelt*

It is amazing the number of people who complain about their lives, believing there is no way they can find happiness with what they have right now. Their values in life is about who has the most toys, and they equate happiness with being rich with an abundance of friends and or being famous and sought after. Their mistake is that happiness begins internally before external gain is added. You must know that if there is breath and life in your body, you begin building inner happiness, joy, and peace. The Bible teaches that the power of life and death is in our tongue! It means what you say matters! Your words form your spiritual world it becomes the foundation of your physical life. You must speak what you want in your life, not what you hate. The Bible says to call things that are not as though they were! (Romans 4:17) So, you speak the changes you want to see.

This process, of course, must move from the spoken word, to the action word, if you are going to see and touch what you say in the spiritual realm come to life in the physical world. Don't pray or speak about things people have acquired in their life or compare your life with theirs. Develop a clear vision of where you want to go and what you want to accomplish. Begin by discovering what you love and start doing that. Try doing at least one thing you love every day,

no matter how small that activity may be. When you begin speaking and nurturing a positive healthy attitude, be sure you surround yourself with people of the same mind and actions. Toxic people poison your efforts every time. These complainers come out of the old you and you no longer need them. Their toxic energy poisons your future and hinders your happiness. Start giving yourself to others; volunteer at your church or a non-profit that you love. These efforts will pull your focus away from you, and putting it on the needs of others will benefit you greatly. Watch less TV, because advertiser's bank on you falling for their lies that you're not good enough or you need to rush out and buy the latest clothes, gadgets, etc. Limiting your exposure to these negative influences

Pastor Sonya Y. Cheltenham

hinders their feeding of your feelings of unhappiness. Look for and appreciate the small things; be positive; choose to be happy and decide to love life!

CHAPTER EIGHT

CONFIDENTLY ME

*"She is clothed with strength and dignity, and she
laughs without fear of the future."*
(Proverbs 31:25, NLT)

Despite what you may have heard about men in the church, or better, men in the Bible, God created men to be confident, secure, and satisfied. Over the centuries of your lives you have digressed from your former self, created in Adam, to rule, have dominion and reproduce. Your Father, Adam had the dignity and strength to stand with Eve and command Eden to become what God said it should be. He was not afraid to speak boldly the things God told him to do and say he succumbed to the lies an unseen enemy told the woman given to him by God.

It appears Adam was sure of his destiny and of his God Who held and created his future. His failure to stand against the lies presented to him by Eve. Since that time, men have been chasing their value and worth, not just with others but worse, within themselves. When trying to become confident, it's important to understand that it has nothing to do with what's on the outside of a person, because confident people care more about what's inside than about their outward appearance.

> *"Keep your eyes open for spiritual danger; stand true to the Lord; act like men; be strong."*
> — *(1 Corinthians 16:13, TLB)*

Have you ever walked by a car window and felt an irresistible urge to check out your reflection, or felt self-conscious all day because of that unwanted blemish right in the middle of your chin, or have that nagging feeling your clothes weren't right? If so, you are aware of one of the universal truths of being a man–no matter what age, how people see you matters to you, sometimes too much.

But another universal truth that the Bible points out in 1 Corinthians 6:13 is that your looks, physique, and people's opinions do not last. Over the course of our lifetime we will gain and lose weight, gain wrinkles, and lose hair. The Bible wants you to see that a spiritually strong man does not have to use his body for attention but will have the kind of attractiveness that makes him true to the Lord, acting like a man while being strong.

It is a relationship with God that makes a man truthful, strong, and confident. His character is defined by who he is with God. His confidence is contagious. What is more attractive and admirable than a man who is unshakeable? His confident strength is not tied to his things, body, or money, but it oozes from the depth of his soul, causing anyone near him to want to know him better. He is the basis of inspiration because his hope is in nothing less than the respect, power, and indwelling of Jesus Christ. He has learned that his joy and inspiration has little to do with external events making him happy, because he relies solely on the joy of the Lord which infuses his strength. You must know that becoming and maintaining the lifestyle of a confident man is not the absence of uneasiness or momentary fear. It is walking in the knowledge that in your weakness God promises to make you strong.

Men who have received the blessing of confidence from God not only inspire other men, but they also inspire the women in their lives. This inspiration comes from them not being desperate for the attention of women but rather compliment them by their style and self-assuredness.

"The Lord says: Cursed is the man who puts his trust in mortal man and turns his heart away from God." (Jeremiah 17:5, *TLB*)

Living to get attention, by comparing and competing with other men will harm the people around you. When you live like this, your motives get twisted, causing you to not look at women for a relationship, but as a means to make you feel better. In turn, you also look at men not as friends, but as competition. The dreadful end is that you are never able to get the relationships you want. The result is, you end up hurting the people around you because you don't view or treat them as people when your only goal is attention.

The good news is, you can stop living for attention and approval by beginning to strive to live for things greater than attention, like a relationship with God which is our greatest step in life, enhancing your relationships with people. It is only then that we no longer feel the need to crave or compete for attention. You have a God-designed purpose, like enriching other people's lives; that's why we create a higher standard for ourselves and no longer live for the purpose of others' approval.

> "I know, GOD, that mere mortals can't run their own lives, That men and women don't have what it takes to take charge of life. So, correct us, GOD, as you see best."
> — *(Jeremiah 10:23-25, MSG)*

Confident men are known for their strength and their ability to shift the center of their world from themselves to God; the results of this is clear in their lives and attitude. When the focus is not on you, the God-given ability makes room in your heart to care about other people, and you reach out seeking to do things for others that you wouldn't have normally done on our own with wide open arms, to help, touch and support others who may never feel this kind of love. The only way you are capable of this kind of selfless strength and confident love is through a solid and daily relationship with God. God knows the great things you can do and be when you are confident and close to Him. You just need to do the spiritual work it takes to become a strong confident man! Investigating the Bible for the strong confident man as we did above help us to pinpoint attributes of a great man. I want to go a little further and look at a few more virtues. The first thing we find shining like a beacon of light is his faith. This strong man is full of faith, so before you attempt to gain any other trait, gain faith. A confident man serves God with all his heart, mind, and soul; he constantly seeks His Will for his decisions and destiny, and he willingly follows God's ways.

The confident man walks in respect and he casts a shadow of respect on everyone who encounters him. If he is married, he loves and respects his wife. If he is dating, his stature and demeanor demands respect from every woman who may want him to pop the question. A married man loves his wife, so he covers, protects, and provides security to her all the days of her life. His wife puts her utmost trust in him because he is a trustworthy person. The single man with this confidence carries himself in a way that available women immediately trust him.

A confident man brings strength and provision when there is a need, but never out of his need to have someone close. The confident man teaches his children the ways of his Father in Heaven. He nurtures them through the love of Christ which includes disciplining them with care and wisdom. The training of his children will be in the way they should go, praying and knowing when they become old, they will not depart from that teaching. Receiving the confidence of God has taught you to love your body and the confident man cares for his body, through eating, exercising and cleanliness. He provides healthy food for himself and his family if he has one. He takes time to exercise to keep his body under control, because he has learned self-control in this book. The confident man is eager to lend a hand wherever it is needed; he serves his wife, family, friends, and neighbors. The confident man touches others with a strong, kind, and gentle spirit exposing the love of God living within him. A virtuous confident man is on top of his finances; he wisely spends his money being careful to purchase quality items needed by his family. This type of man has an entrepreneurial spirit enabling him to look toward the future with the wisdom of God,

Who gives him the power to gain wealth to increase the seed he has placed in his life. He is willing to engage in education and training to improve his state and place in life with confidence that his efforts will not go unrewarded. This man's home does not have to be rich, but he works with his hands to create an atmosphere of warmth, peace and love for himself, his family, friends, and guests. His confident use of hospitality ministers to everyone around him; visitors love coming to his home and have a hard time leaving. This confident strong man is wise with time; he redeems it to diligently complete his daily exploits. He plans ahead to store what he needs during prosperous times to cover himself when times become lean. He understands the value of time and uses it wisely by not spending time dwelling on those things that do not please the Lord. This confident man knows his worth and strength. He is not stuck on superficial things on the inside, but he lives by an inner code of strength, integrity, and truth that can only come from Jesus Christ. He uses his creativity, visionary abilities and sense of style to create strength and security in and around his life. Because this is his inner code (passion) he works to bring this strength to the lives of countless others. The traits of this man are not for you to disqualify yourself and to throw in the towel, but all of us need a rule and guide to measure where we are. That is the purpose of it being in the Bible.

This man worked hard for these traits to be evident in his life. I don't believe he was born with them, but he had to come to them beginning with his faith and trust in God. You, too have been destined to become this confident man. Begin it with faith, the good ground and basis of all the other traits mentioned above. This is a guide for you to ensure that you grow and because you have chosen to read this book. I know you are growing; it is my desire that you grow in the right direction. Before you begin your investment in any of the other traits, begin it in God. As you begin spending time in prayer and reading His Word, you become more like him and all the other traits begin to show themselves in your life. The way he dressed spoke to his confidence and destiny. He made sure he wasn't caught up in the latest fad, but that he determined his way. He walked in the direction he wanted to go speaking the things that weren't in his life yet as though they were already his. Your confidence is waiting for you; do not sit there waiting for something to happen. Believe by faith that God ordained this destiny just for you and begin to walk in it because your steps forward are ordered by your God. This confident man knows he is a son of the One True King Jesus and he is not shamed or embarrassed about it. He has integrity and character that makes him great from the inside out. It's not always about having a lot of money to buy the finest things; it's the state of your heart and mind that will get you where money can't take you. He is so confident that he laughs in the face of fear. You may ask how I can laugh when the bills are due, and I don't have enough money to make this month's mortgage. It is because you know in Whom you trust, and this is another opportunity for your God to show Himself strong in your life.

> *"Do you think it's possible in broad daylight to enter the house of an awake, able-bodied man, and walk off with his possessions unless you tie him up first? Tie him up, though, and you can clean him out."*
> *— (Mark 3:27, MSG)*

You may not understand how things are going to work out, but have the boldest of confidence in your Lord and Savior Jesus Christ, because the same way He took care of the sparrows, He can take care of you. A confident man puts his complete trust and faith in his God, which makes it impossible to overthrow him. He may be knocked down but with trust and faith, he always gets up again.

Have you ever met someone, and it seemed as if every word that came out of their mouth was like honey; it just gave you life? Have you ever left a conversation empowered and ready to take on the world? This is the type of man God wants you to be, a man of virtue and integrity as stated before. God wants you to inspire other men to empower them. It's time to start building each other up. So, finding a mentor with these qualities will help you have accountability while you cultivate the above stated characteristics. Let's take a few moments do take a closer look at the Word of God. His description is either daunting to you or unreachable! The question is what God had really intended for us to take away from the principles described in the passage. Let's see!

I really love the man described in the Bible. 'Listen,' I thought, as I envisioned men organizing their lives in such a way that they could be as amazing as he was to me. After giving prolonged thought to this amazing model of a Christian man, I became intimidated by him. One thing I learned in dissecting his qualities and pulling them into the 21st century is that he could be any man, not just a married man, any man living anywhere in the world. That ah-ha moment made me realize this important piece while pulling the positive qualities out of this great man's description. We don't want to get stuck on the details unless it is customary in your personal culture to sit at the gate to be praised, herd sheep and keep servants.

This list was customary for the city and culture at that time. How you apply the value of these Scriptures will be within the context of your culture and customs. The Bible teaches that this man can be trusted! Not only can he be trusted, he is trustworthy. A trustworthy person's past behavior, attitude and conduct is worthy of everyone's trust. Most of us know someone or a few people who fit in this category. This characteristic is one that we must all seek to emulate. Trust is the cousin of respect. Respect is what most men yearn for and seek in relationships with others, especially women. For a man to practice this characteristic means he is establishing for himself a character trait that others will seek. Being trustworthy brings great benefit to those who practice this art. It is a trait that draws anyone seeking a person of safety and security to you.

> *"Then this humanlike figure touched me again and gave me strength. He said, 'Don't be afraid, friend. Peace. Everything is going to be all right. Take courage. Be strong.'*
>
> *"Even as he spoke, courage surged up within me. I said, 'Go ahead, let my master speak. You've given me courage.'"*
> — *Daniel 10:18, 19, MSG)*

This man was on top of his game! He knew where his strength came from. His business was touched; his life was touched, and he wasn't afraid to go far and wide to accomplish his task. He looked for the best, the best items and the best price, not the most expensive. He was a wise and sharp shopper and always worked for the good of his family. He was tight and frugal when vision goals were trying to be reached. This man learned what was needed to be a successful entrepreneur. Have you done what was necessary to promote that dream into a vision? Have you gone the extra mile and then some to become all that God has called and anointed you to be? Dissecting this model shows you where you must seek greater width or longer length to be who we were created to be! Don't cut yourself short or settle for something too small to contain your greatness. God has touched you and perfect love casts out all fear! Go the extra mile; get up an hour earlier and stay up an hour longer. This small adjustment could mean the success you're working for is one that fits the greatness in you. Following the pattern of the biblical man may mean your life will be cut the right way, to fit only you, in all the right places. The New Century Version of the Bible states:

> *"I say this because I know what I am planning for you," says the Lord. "I have good plans for you, not plans to hurt you. I will give you hope and a good future."*
> *— (Jeremiah 29:11, NCV)*

He is a true entrepreneur; he works the plan of God so the plan works for him. He researched investments for the greatest possible returns and when he finds it, he buys it. It doesn't matter whether its land, stocks, savings, bonds, or other investments, the strong man is up and about his business. The Scripture implies he not only finds good investments he develops what he invests in, because God has promised to give him hope and a good future. This man commands his day. He rises with expectations that the day will respond to his expectations. He gets up early with plans for his day. He is not afraid to put in the necessary work and then some to accomplish his goals and vision.

> *"Be alert. Continue strong in the faith. Have courage and be strong."*
> *—(1 Corinthians 16:13, NCV)*

Another trait worth emulating from this character is that he was purposeful and savvy; he acquired skill in what was needed in his time. He didn't wait for things to come to him, but he went out of his way to seize every moment for all it could give him, and he was the type that squeezed out any left over. He kept his own place up not allowing laziness to creep in leaving things to go undone. He used his learned abilities to make his home safe and clean while taking his family shopping in places that did not break his budget. He was great with finances. This man was so diligent and sure of himself he was willing to practice self-sacrifice by helping anyone he found in need. He didn't wait for people to ask for help but he reached out to the poor, even if it meant putting their needs before his needs.

> *"Anyone who speaks should speak words from God. Anyone who serves should serve with the strength God gives so that in everything God will be praised through Jesus Christ. Power and glory belong to him forever and ever. Amen."*
> *— (1 Peter 4:11, NCV)*

This passage sums up most of this premise about men. He was a man of wisdom as seen in his character traits and actions and as heard throughout the Bible. These Scriptures are admonishing you as men that whatever you seek and whatever you gain in this life, wisdom is the principle thing. The book of Proverbs celebrates wisdom in action and is not a rule of action for just women, but a list of character traits that serves extremely well anyone exercising them. This poem was written primarily to men and it is instructive to them as the poem suggests, "Praise her for all her hands have done." In the Jewish custom, men sing this poem to their wives, sisters, daughters, and mothers to bring them honor and praise for having these types of characteristics. We as Christians must take care not to interpret this passage as prescriptive or a command to women rather than an ode to women of this level of character. In the Christian world, the passage is no longer a poem that men offer as a praise of women rather a task list through which a woman earns her place of value. I believe our present position is in error and misses the intended point of the poem. Remember, this virtuous woman or woman of valor isn't so much about what you do. It's more about how you do and ultimately about how you feel about what you're doing that registers as you "Matter!" When you do things with valor, intentionality and love, that's what makes you a man or woman of character that the world desires. The point of the discussion is that it is about characters that honor, and not rules that tear down.

CHAPTER NINE

MENTORS AND OTHER NEEDED THINGS

"Therefore encourage one another and build each other up ..."

— (1Thessalonians 5:11, NIV)

Mentoring is a biblical idea; it began in the Bible and the Bible gives great examples of how men are called to mentor each other. Yes, it is true, the word "mentor" is not used in Scripture; but the principles and skills applied when using this terminology are found throughout the entire biblical text. We see excellent examples of mentoring relationships taking place throughout the Bible. When you read through the Bible, you will notice in some cases that some individuals were involved in multiple mentoring relationships. There are mentors at your fingertips for differing issues in your life. Sometimes these mentoring sessions happened on a one-to-one basis, and in other cases, it took place in a group. However, when

165

seeking a mentor or group make sure the group is always small enough to listen to and interact with everyone who joins.

Jesus, our perfect example, mentored 12, sometimes three, and on rare occasions, one. It was Jesus' intent to ensure that not one of his mentees was falling into error for lack of direction. It is important that you know the purpose for meeting a mentor. This is not some fly-by-night gathering, or a hanging session, where someone is talking off the top of their head uttering illogical rhetoric expecting you to follow through. The important thing is that this is a God-ordained connection built out of love for the growth and destiny of you, the mentee. We can each be that person who welcomes the assurance of the hope we have in the Lord Jesus Christ, or we can be the one who offers that same assurance to another. You can work to be a loving, supportive member of a strong mentoring relationship. When you hear of a mentoring relationship like Jethro mentoring Moses, you learn that these types of relationships are God-ordained. To establish a good mentoring encounter the foundation or beginning is to establish a close relationship. Moses and Jethro had this through marriage because Jethro was Moses' father-in-law. In the book of Exodus, it describes the way these two men interacted with each other and from that interaction we summarize their relationship is friendly. Exodus 18:1-8 tells us that the men greeted one another and seemed to be concerned with each other's welfare. It also indicates they spent time together talking and discussing the events in their lives. Be sure not to overly focus on the mentoring and miss the relationship. When the mentor and mentee fail to develop a relationship built on trust, mutual respect, and commitment the mentoring will not work. The next important foundation that mentoring relationships must be based on is transparency. This same passage shows us Moses' willingness to share his situation with Jethro. Moses had to be feeling overwhelmed with being responsible for over a million people, displaced from the place they called home for 400 years. Admittedly, it was an awful situation of servitude they were fleeing from; it had its dysfunction of being home. Moses told his father-in-law everything the Lord had done and said to him. He was willing to be vulnerable with Jethro, admitting his fears, weaknesses, mistakes, and concerns. I believe Jethro was also willing to be transparent with Moses. The third important foundation of a mentoring relationship is the mentor must genuinely desire the best for his protégé as in Exodus 18:9-12 which reveals that Jethro was happy and excited with how God used Moses and blessed him. They shared their mutual commitment to God, and Jethro knew Moses' victory was victory for him also. The passage seems to suggest that Jethro was a little bit more excited than Moses. Jethro prepared a party and huge feast for Moses and all the leaders of Israel. Mentors must be willing to celebrate the successes of their mentees; it is part of the reason they mentor and they should be the mentee's number one cheerleader! The next foundation is that mentors make rich positive investments in the lives of those being mentored. According to Exodus 18:13-23, Moses was a new leader that lacked the leadership skills needed to properly lead his people. He was a great general in a time of crisis, but he suffered with overseeing the daily affairs of his people. Not unlike leaders today, Moses had to learn that different seasons of leadership require different leadership skills. A mentor's job is to continue developing those being trained by seeing the times, praying and knowing what to do. Moses, like leaders today, tried to do everything himself; he did all the judging, all the counseling, all the directing and all the planning! I'm not sure why. It could have been since God spoke directly to Moses, he may have felt it was solely his responsibility. Maybe it was his lack of trust that others would do it like him. Maybe it was ignorance or overestimating his own importance. Whatever may be summarized, it is obvious Moses felt he was doing the right thing. Like many leaders do, he made spiritual excuses for why he had not trained or mentored others.

Jethro stepped in and helped Moses develop as a leader and then train others. Jethro questioned Moses' methods in Exodus 18:14, then pointed why those methods were not working and were not good for Moses nor the people. He showed Moses that his efforts were hindering the effectiveness of God's people. Jethro stepped up and offered his wisdom to Moses. He suggested that Moses stop judging, stop representing all the people, stop being the only spokesman for God to the people, or stop teaching all the classes on God's laws and how to live. Jethro didn't just say stop! He developed a strategic practical solution for Moses. Jethro instructed Moses to choose from the people, able men of integrity and character to help, and let those men help with judging. As a result of Jethro's mentoring and Moses willingness to be mentored, things became easier for Moses and the people were better served. Jethro's commitment to positively investing in others was useful in building the people of Israel, just as leaders following a strong mentor builds better ministry. It's all about building the ministry of mentorship to build people. Mentoring therefore is only possible if you are teachable. If you are trying to save face, unwilling to be transparent, or trying to keep a macho image for the public, you will miss the positive benefits of mentorship. Moses heard what his father-in-law said and did exactly what he was told. Oh yes, there were many reasons he could have disregarded his father-in-law, but due to his meekness and humility he followed wise counsel. The fact that he listened and obeyed showed Moses was teachable. He did not think he had arrived or that he needed to wait for God to speak directly to him, when God had sent wise counsel through his father-in-law.

It doesn't matter if it is a marriage relationship, or a sacred friendship or a mentorship, they will become foundational to your life and growth only if God is kept in the center.

A quote from *30 Essential Lessons from Women of the Bible*, by Kimbriah L. Alfrenar, published by Freeman-Smith, says it so well:

> "God does not intend that you experience mediocre relationships. He created you for far greater things. Building lasting relationships requires compassion, wisdom, empathy, kindness, courtesy, perseverance, and forgiveness. If it sounds like a lot of work, it is – which is perfectly fine with God. Why? Because He knows you are capable of doing that work and because He knows that the fruits of your labors will enrich the lives of your loved ones and the lives of generations unborn."

I cannot stress enough the importance of you connecting with a mentor or joining a group where mentoring takes place. Regardless of how people may view mentoring, it is a biblical idea. These Scriptural references aren't necessarily meant to show that young adults desire relationships of this nature because they want to follow the biblical model. However, emerging generations recognize almost naturally that they have a lot to learn, and the Bible affirms a relationship model that can be used to meet that need. So, you may want to know what a mentor can do for you. Why is it useful for you to engage in a mentoring relationship? A successful mentoring relationship focuses on the progress, growth, and success of the mentee. The guidance of the mentor is best served when it addresses the mentee's present life needs. A keen mentor will listen and learn, asking the mentee questions to uncover where the mentee would like to go and what they would like to learn. After making this type of connection, the mentor serves as a guide toward the desired end. The misconception that the mentor must be a scholar spewing an abundance of knowledge on any given subject, or have a thorough knowledge of the Bible, discourages many from stepping up to mentor young people seeking directions for their lives. When we consider the term "guides," we learn that they are people familiar with the path you're on because they have traveled that way before. A guide's purpose is to assist anyone traveling the path they are familiar with offering them information about their own travels and warning the mentees of impending dangers. They also offer aid when things have gone wrong. The goal of the Christian mentor is to change lives through the application of biblical truths. Your role as a mentee is not to sit passively by and allow someone to direct your destiny, but to partner with the mentor in a learning process through discussions. So, be sure to bring all your questions to contribute to the knowledge you will be gaining. This reciprocal relationship flows from mentor to mentee when it is effective and free, primarily focusing on advancing the mentee toward their destiny. Authentic mentorship happens when both parties share real-life experiences, not just successes but the good, the bad, and the ugly that may have produced brokenness and then healing. Mentee's yearn for honesty from their mentors who are willing to share their mistakes and the grace they received to recover. When a mentor is this transparent, it increases the faith, hope, and strength of the mentee. As a potential mentee, you must be careful that you do not approach this relationship with unrealistic expectations. The mentor should not be expected to meet your personal needs, and they may be unable to meet all your mentee needs as well. When you approach the relationship with these types of expectations, it will put a strain on the relationship and may cause it to end. When you find the group or person you would like to work with, be sure you have done your homework on where you are trying to go and what you want to accomplish through this relationship. Ensure your interactions are intentional and valuable or both of you will lose interest. Finally, both you and the mentor must establish rules of confidentiality to ensure mutual trust, because if trust is lost it is almost impossible to reestablish it. The Bible gives us the groundwork for intentionally developing friendships among differing generations. It speaks to men investing in the lives of each other through encouragement, guidance, listening, sharing, laughing, and strengthening each other. The goal of these relationships is to form strong mentoring bonds and lasting relationship between men who are willing to be a source of support, strength, and growth to other men. This circle of support is vital for your continued growth and healing. If there is one thing I have learned over the thirty plus years in my career is that many of my accomplishments, and the good things I experienced, were rarely accomplished alone. Most of my successes were securely connected to getting the right advice and backing from the right person or people. Throughout all our lives we have had the benefit of mentors, even if we didn't realize it. For many of us, our mentors were our parents, grandparents, and other family members, not to mention peers, teachers, and pastors. Every great craftsman learned their craft from a leader in their area. Having the right mentor means connecting to someone who has accomplished what you're trying to accomplish. They have walked that path and know the sacrifices and pitfalls to avoid for you to be successful. Many look for mentors who have connections like a "good 'ole boys' network." I know and believe these relationships are so much more than that. Mentors can teach you skills and give you sound advice for your specific field. Mentors can boost your self-esteem like no other relationships can. When a healthy relationship has been established with a mentor, you have given them power to speak into your life. They then can encourage, empower, guide, and give requested guidance for your pending goals. Often, for men, you are your worst enemy. You criticize yourselves beyond what others think. You drag childhood issues into your adult life; and you disqualify yourselves before you try. Men, lacking a father image, or a positive male image, hinder their progress toward their destiny. Due to this negative influence, men tend to begin thinking they cannot, but will act as if they can, until someone tells them they can and/or tells them they are doing a good job. It is clear, by watching and listening to men, that they too fight a sense of subservience that was deeply planted into their minds from childhood, and centuries of programmed beliefs have been hard to change or shake. However, men have had great success in working their way out from under centuries of believing this way. The work of changing this type of belief becomes easier when the guidance of a trusted mentor is brought into the task. This valuable partnership could mean a man can overcome internal and external factors that have been hindering his progress. You may ask, how do I find a good mentor? I'm so glad you asked. Finding a mentor begins with you. Start thinking of people you admire for their achievements and industry experience. Maybe someone you know has had great success with a mentor and offers you their contact information. Remember, your mentor should be someone who shares your professional, ministry, family, and personal outlook. Even better if they have accomplished the goals you hope to attain. Think through your list of people you truly believe you will gain something from. Before you ask that person to mentor you, invite them to coffee, or lunch and pick their brain about their experiences to get the best idea of how your relationship with them will work.

Take your time; you will want your mentor to be supportive, communicative, and inspiring, and they must feel that your needs are important. Get to know the person well. Build a relationship with them so that you are comfortable with sharing your life, struggles and issues with them. If you don't know someone off hand, look for someone connected to the community, who is involved in your church or club. They seem to be people involved with life and making changes with people. Remember, a mentor isn't someone who tells you what to do but someone who encourages you to find your own answers. Your job as a mentee is being willing to be open to new ideas, act on the guidance given, and be prepared to adapt and change. Accessing a mentor can cause fear because they will try to pull you out of your comfort zone if it means greater success for you. It is good and good for you to move in that direction; you will be better because of it. Mentoring is an intentional ministry designed to develop friendships where men invest in the lives of other men through guidance, listening, laughing and strengthening them toward the accomplishment of their goals. These mentors are usually wise men of faith and godly conduct. This type of mentor offers a spiritually sound and safe environment of all men. Once you determine if your mentor is for professional guidance or spiritual guidance or both, you need to make an agreement or contract for the length of time you will invest in your meetings. You and your mentor may speak weekly or meet monthly; the schedule should work for both of you.

CHAPTER TEN

FEAR: THE ENEMY IN ME

———————— ୬୧୬୧ ————————

Fear in and of itself has a purpose. When you're in a scary situation, like you walk upon a lion, it's understandable that you know what you're feeling and why! You're afraid, because you're confronted with a definite threat to your life! So, your feelings of fear are meant to keep you safe; it causes you to quickly get away from what's causing the fear, as fast as you can. Fear causes us to take action. The lion stops and looks at you at the very moment you're looking at him. Fear sends adrenaline shooting through your veins; your heart is pumping blood so fast it feels as if it will jump out of your chest! You're dripping with sweat as you try to figure out if you should run or stay still. As your body tingles all over, you feel a sharp jolt and you find yourself sitting in your own bed, with your body and hair wet from the sweat of a dream that seems more like reality then anything you have experienced before. The symptoms of fear work the same in your dreams as they do in real life. On the other hand, understanding fear when it comes to relationships is harder to identify, because it's not that you're in fear for your life, is it? And, although you cannot pinpoint the threat, it is very real and just as valid. This type of fear is called the "fear of intimacy." The basis of fear is to keep you safe; however, when its connected to establishing intimate relationships, it will keep you from being close, loving and connected. It shows itself in differing ways. Let's discuss a few of them.

FEAR OF BEING ABANDONED

Loving relationships involve risks; both parties must be willing to be vulnerable to have a committed relationship. From the moment you commit to being in a loving relationship with someone you live with the risk of being left. That daily struggle can be very scary. The thought of opening your heart and allowing someone in, then dealing with the possibility of being left is an inward weight of fear. Although you believe you trust him or her, there is that constant nervous pain in the pit of your stomach. There is a clear and present threat that the relationship may not work out. That threat is the pain of heartbreak. The threat becomes especially terrifying if you have waited, searched, and planned for the "real deal," "Ms. Candy Cane," the woman of your dreams! You have been careful about who and what you want. It has taken a long time causing you not to be able to bear the thought of another relationship not working out. Fear is doing its job by trying to keep you safe from the feelings that cause you to not venture into the valley of risk. Prior to this relationship, you dealt with people from a distance. You just don't get too close. So you tell yourself, 'You keep a safe distance and you won't have to worry about being afraid,' or so your mind reassures you. Natural normal fear gives our bodies what they need to escape or survive life-threatening situations. The fear that causes you to not enjoy life and live life to the fullest is not from God; it is from our enemy, Satan, according to 2 Timothy 1:7. Fear is the king of all the spirits that try to hold us back; it is the spirit Satan uses to rule and run the lives of God's people. He uses it with skill and success keeping God's people from coming under God's leadership. There are a great number of people who never fulfill the call of God on their lives simply because every time they move forward, the spirit of fear raises its ugly head and causes them to retreat, letting go of their resolve to move out in faith. Living with fear can be tormenting and keep you from enjoying life.

The second type of fear we need to discuss is:

FEAR OF BEING SMOTHERED

One thing we all admit is that being single comes with a lot of freedom. You decide what you do, or don't do with your time. Your choices and priorities are based only on your feelings. The idea of a close committed relationship presents its own issues and problems for your sense of freedom. Even though you want a genuine, lasting, and loving relationship, part of you may be afraid that having this relationship is going to take away your freedom. Some counselors call this "The common other half mentality," which leads you to fears about getting into a committed relationship. This theory teaches that you are incomplete until you find a partner, causing you to feel like you must compromise a great deal to gain one. The compromise could include the potential loss of individuality, autonomy, and personal space. The thing with fighting internal fear is that both types of fear tend to take hold of you at the same time.

We genuinely want to be in a relationship, but we are also equally afraid of being left AND of losing ourselves. Your only choice is to free yourself from the fear that's keeping love at a distance. It's no wonder why finding a great partner and creating a healthy relationship feels like a shot in the dark. Once you confront and get rid of these fears, the chains that held you back come crashing to the ground, and their effects are no longer running your life. Only then will you be open to love flowing into your life so fast you won't want to stop it. In fighting fear, remember this spirit is not from God. Every time you are feeling fearful about stepping out or stepping up to where God has called you, fear comes from our enemy and it is a manifestation of his kingdom which is darkness. This is the spirit that Satan uses to control people who love God, paralyzing them from living in the light and love of their Savior, Jesus Christ. Joy and gladness in the Lord have the power to overcome fear. The Bible teaches the joy of the Lord is our strength! We can overcome fearful moments by allowing the loving joy of Jesus Christ to fill every inch of our soul and spirit. When we take our concerns to God, there in his presence we find fullness of joy, and out of the provision of His right hand we can receive pleasures forever (Psalm 16:11). We can walk in the freedom He has designed for us; however, we must meet Him daily to receive joy and pleasure because His mercies are renewed every morning (Lamentations 3:22, 23). This is our place of hope, that regardless of what's happening in our circumstances or the circle where we stand, we can willfully walk out of the chaos of that circle into the intimacy of

Christ to receive the strength of joy in trouble, and joy in sorrow, knowing that our times are in His hands.

We have all read psychological distress is not good for us. Researchers are now reporting fear and psychological distress may cause us cancer which increases our death rates. When thinking about the connection of fear and faith we cannot overlook the number of people in Scripture who found divine strength in the most fearful times. Here are just a few, Daniel in the lion's den, Paul in the Philippian jail, Moses standing before the Red Sea, Peter and John on trial before the Sanhedrin. We could go on and find there are so many others we could name. Each one looked death in the eye, and yet each found the faith to trust God with their fears. We must all learn not to "fear the fear." The devil brings fear, but we have been given power by our loving Savior to not give in to fear.

In the book of Psalms, David said, *"What time I am afraid, I will trust in thee."* (Psalm 56:3) Whenever God leads us to step out in an area to do something new and exciting or to step up to a greater commitment, normally we feel fear. However, if God truly is leading you in this direction, you have the power to choose to trust Him. The time is now to face your fear by confronting what has held you back and stymied your movements. Your desire to be free will fuel you overcoming your fear. If you are in this fight, let me encourage you to get help and support, if needed, and take Jesus' hand and go forward with what He is trying to move you to.

What can we learn from the life of these great people? Faith is a life prayer God empowers.

Scripture teaches us, *"Do not be anxious about anything, but in everything by prayer and supplication with thanksgiving let your requests be made known to God."* (Philippians 4:6, *ESV*) God wants us to *"Be strong and courageous,"* (Deuteronomy 31:6, *NIV*) as He instructed Moses to tell us. We can stand on these instructions even in our lowest moments because when life is too heavy, we have the privilege to *"Cast all your anxieties on (God), because he cares for you."* (1 Peter 5:7)

God never asks more of us then He has equipped us to handle. What He has asked us to do, He has enabled us to do just what He says. The secret is not in our trying harder to get it right, or to be approved or even to do better. It is the ability to humbly admit we are afraid and ask God for the faith we lack. Then God will walk in and overcome our issues and challenges. He works them for our good by causing them to build our faith and courage. There is nothing Satan hates more than having what he meant for evil used for our good.

So, gain courage and let's make the enemy mad at us today and every day by naming our fears and claiming the strength of God to trust Him enough to use them for our good. Knowing that God is your ever-present help in your time of need, ask Him without reservation for everything you need. God does not love our martyrs of old more than us. He fought for them; He will do the same for you. What is the "Joy of the Lord?" One thing we can be sure of is God's joy is not the joy of circumstances or temperament. People who do not know God can be joyful over winning the lottery, getting a promotion, going on a fun trip, or enjoying good health. These things would also make a Christian very happy, but the joy of the Lord is something that only those who know the Lord can enjoy, despite circumstances, failures, hurts and pains. We have a great example of the joy of the Lord through the life of King David, because the book of Psalms is full of rejoicing and gladness at times when he endured the most difficulty. There are many, many times in the book of Psalms that tell us that it's not only possible, but necessary for all those who have received God's love and salvation to experience the joy of the Lord. Even though it goes against everything human, your feelings and emotions, it is not natural; it is supernatural. Some may have to work at it harder than others because we have practiced reacting to circumstances with anything other than joy. God has given you a daily supply of joy through His mercy, which is renewed every morning. This type of joy is the joy that God Himself expresses. The God-type of joy is revealed through His love for us when He sent His only son to rescue us from the hands of His enemy. In Hebrews 12:2, it describes that if we look closely at Jesus, we will notice that He endured the pain of the cross while despising the shame of it all. Being innocent Himself from the blame of sin, He took the putdown, hurt and death for us all because of the joy and His intended destination with God.

FEAR NOT!

God does not beat around the bush with this command; He simply tells us don't be afraid! You may ask how we stop feeding our fear and just how, Lord, do we overcome it? Fear grabs our heart and gets our attention. The normal responses of most people to fear is either fight or flight. It doesn't matter if you mask your fear with a strong exterior or a macho bravado, or shy away seeking refuge behind anything close enough to hide you and offer refuge. Fear pushes in on our thinking, decisions, and actions. I have learned there is healthy fear and it is designed to keep us from harm. This type of fear keeps you from burning your hands on a hot stove or grill or running through a red light at a stop. This type of fear is useful and helpful to all of us. But the fear we're discussing keeps us from doing what we want to do, or what we need to do or worse, what God has called us to do. Sometimes fear pushes us into making wrong or dangerous decisions; it can even cause us to disobey God's law. Fear is a problem in our world, neighborhoods, and homes. It is easy to see why many people believe they are living in a fear zone. Politicians, news media, and our American culture play on our fears for their own personal benefit, but it doesn't mean the underlying dangers are not real.

We have global terrorism, mass shootings, pandemics, and warfare spreading in unlikely places. There are mass shootings of the innocent, violent crimes on our streets, epidemics of diseases, natural disasters, and deadly animals impacting us daily through our phones, computers, and TVs. These fearful events are often in our entertainment and seep into our nightmares. The truth is, most of these things we fear will never happen to us. But our anxieties over them and worries about them generally has done nothing to protect us from these impending dangers. The Bible does not minimize these things we fear. The truth is it warns us that the world will become more dangerous and frightening as the end times approach. So how do we obey God's command? Through faith we must believe that God does not want us to be debilitated by fear. This is what the Lord said:

- *"Fear not, for I am with you; Be not dismayed, for I am your God. I will strengthen you, Yes, I will help you, I will uphold you with My righteous right hand." (Isaiah 41:10, NKJV)*

- *"All your children shall be taught by the LORD, And great shall be the peace of your children. In righteousness you shall be established; You shall be far from oppression, for you shall not fear; And from terror, for it shall not come near you." (Isaiah 54:13, 14, NKJV)*
- *"Behold, I am the LORD, the God of all flesh. Is there anything too hard for Me?" (Jeremiah 32:27, NKJV)*
- *"Are not two sparrows sold for a copper coin? And not one of them falls to the ground apart from your Father's will. But the very hairs of your head are all numbered. Do not fear; therefore, you are of more value than many sparrows." (Matthew 10:29-31, NKJV)*
- *"Do not fear, little flock, for it is your Father's good pleasure to give you the kingdom." (Luke 12:32, NKJV)*
- *"Peace I leave with you, My peace I give to you; not as the world gives do I give to you. Let not your heart be troubled, neither let it be afraid." (John 14:27, NKJV)*
- *"For He Himself has said, 'I will never leave you nor forsake you.' So we may boldly say: 'The LORD is my helper; I will not fear. What can man do to me?'" (Hebrews 13:5, 6, NKJV)*

We are invited by God to cast all your cares on Him because He cares for you. We can ask God for peace amid our storms. The work of overcoming fear is first differentiating prudence, godly fear, and sinful fear. Let's begin with prudence, which is defined as wisdom, common sense, or good judgement. Prudence is not just the practice of wisdom by making wise choices but it's the art of avoiding evil. Gaining the skills to practice prudence will help you avoid choices that usher in fear. The Bible describes a prudent person as someone who is sensible about what they attempt in life. They consider their steps and the consequences of these steps. It further suggests that a prudent person surrounds themselves with like-minded people who love knowledge and who avoid evil, unlike a foolish person who continues in a naïve manner in the face of issues, and suffer the consequences of their bad choices. They live their lives surrounded by like-minded people who enjoy discussing their issues and problems but lack the wisdom to make life-altering changes. Like our parents have often said, "Please use the brain God has so graciously given to you." What my Mom was saying is, you don't want to sneak upon a tiger and make it angry. In the same way, you want to be sensible about your purpose and your direction in life to be sure to avoid hurt, harm and danger. God is telling us through His Word that by applying what He said, along with godly common sense, is the only way to live and avoid trouble. The next area in our review of fear is the good type of fear, or what we call godly fear. Godly fear is reverential respect for our salvation through Jesus Christ and all that He is forming us to be. We show reverence and godly fear by our thoughts, words, and deeds coming in line with what He has instructed us to do in the Scriptures. Godly fear gives us the motivation to glorify God in all our ways, by acknowledging that without Him, nothing we put our hands on will be successful. From the small mindless things we engage in like eating and drinking, to the difficulties of relationships with God and mankind, in all these things we acknowledge God reverently as being in charge. The Bible clearly tells us that in everything we do to focus on things above, meaning those things that concern God.

It's like the marketing movement of "What would Jesus do?" Develop the habit of posing this question to every decision in your life. God is clearly saying to focus your mind, heart, and eyes on the things of God, and not on earthly things causing you to fear man more than God. We must go a step further when we discuss the fear of the Lord, because Scripture also tells us that perfect love casts out all fear and the beginning of wisdom is the fear of the Lord. I was taught as a child, there is nothing scarier than God! Don't get me wrong; my parents didn't want me constantly looking around in a state of fear that our God was some boogie man hiding in wait of my first wrong move to pounce on me! They wanted me to know He loved me, but they wanted me wise enough to know with all that's happening in the world, their threats are temporary but

the promises of God are eternal. On a personal level God threatens your ego, your delusions about yourself, because He confronts us with truth and stands against these enemies of your freedom until He has set you free. This love/hate thing has its roots in what God is destroying in you, so He can lift you up to Him. William D. Eisenhower said in *Christianity Today*, "Fear of the Lord is the beginning of wisdom, but love from the Lord is its completion." If I walk in godly fear, nothing and no one is stronger or more powerful than He is. Who is left for us to fear?!

In 2008, my precious daughter was diagnosed with a rare form of breast cancer. Hearing that news sent fear through my entire body, even as the enemy worked against my imagination through the corners of my mind. Everywhere I looked, north, south, east, and west, seemed off base, unsure, and lacking a foundation to hold on to. It was a downright scary time. The news of her illness stabbed my heart like a two-edge sword, cutting into every aspect of my life at the very moment my daughter gave us this devastating news. I remember her phone call like it was yesterday. "Mom," she said. That 'Mom' was filled with more desperation than I had heard from her before. Hearing the emotion in her voice I demanded, "What's wrong?" as she struggled to find the words to tell me, her Mom, about the pending darkness soon to overcome us. I remember the long pregnant pause she took to explain how they came to their conclusion. I felt fear for her and fear with her as our two-year journey for her physical life began. After accepting the need to fight against this killer called cancer, I went into prayer and asked God to forgive my worry and unbelief. I had to declare through tear-stained eyes my belief that whatever His decision was with my daughter's life was good with me. After acknowledging my weakness, and my willingness to embrace the man-made fear associated with this diagnosis, I felt a peace that passed my understanding, subdued my logic, and left me helpless in the face of the facts. Even as I watched the gift of physical life leave my daughter, and the presence of eternal life invade her room, I knew we were accompanied with the warmth and presence of perfect love. He gently overshadowed us with an unreasonable peace which ruled my broken heart. Even in great sorrow, there was a peace that grew from the reverence of Who God is that passed my understanding and left medical logic helpless.

The fear God warned us about in His command "Fear Not" can be considered sinful fear. This fear pulls us away from the biblical teaching on how we should think, speak, live, and behave. The easiest ways to determine if your fear is sinful or godly is by asking if your behavior will bring glory and honor to God. That includes what you do and what you refuse to do! When we get caught up in sinful fear, it usually has its roots in our desire for the approval of others, and our desire to control our life or situation instead of bringing ourselves into the discipline of living out God's Word and principles for us. We are God's greatest creations and He hardwired us with various emotions and thoughts. With this, none of us are expected to never fear or worry. We are, however, expected to seek and follow the example of Christ by again asking ourselves, "What would Jesus do?" Even in seeking God's face we must still choose to obey and follow Him. So, what do you do to ensure you get it right? First, begin with prayer. Don't forget to include rejoicing and being thankful, and boldly make your request known to God. We must cultivate right thinking by disciplining our mind. This discipline will ensure you do not fall for the tricks of the devil. This ability comes from meditating on God's Word. The next step is our behavior. We must "behave out" or "act out" our belief! We have to live what we believe is true. This step ushers us into the peace God gives, not worldly peace that's based on situations, but God's peace that's based on Who He is and what He has the power to do. This peace will bring you to worship instead of worry, to faith instead of flight and to stand instead of tremble. This is the place God is calling you to. What we should understand is that godly fear chases fleshly fear; it subdues our concern that we can't be good enough or that we don't matter. It wrestles down the thoughts that we will never measure up to God's requirements or His expectations. The reality is that we will never be good enough and we can never fill the bill or requirements of God. But the good news is that Jesus measured up and was more than enough when He paid it all for us.

Therefore, we are made whole and complete through Him, which is enabling us to come boldly before the presence of God since we are no longer slaves, but sons and daughters of God. He views our shortcomings considering Who Jesus is and sees us as righteous, able, and more than enough, only because of Jesus' sacrifice. So godly fear is loving and trusting Him enough to live your life, not based on what others think, but in the "Son light" of Who Jesus is! Godly fear is loving and trusting that God won't hurt you. God wants you to know that He's not like your other lovers. You gave yourself to them and they hurt you and took advantage of you. In you, God sees Himself, a real reflection of His expectations for every one of us. You living out God's design is you giving back to Him what He has put inside of you. When He returns that love, it is a far greater love than you have given Him. As we look to Jesus for our living and our being, we begin to build a solid foundation of self-approval that we can stand on. We must be sure that we are not only behaving reverently but that our hearts come to know God intimately. This transformation begins in our souls so that the outward expression reflects the inward condition.

Being told not to fear is easier said than done if the person telling you is struggling with similar life issues and fears. Fear has a way of creeping into the smallest situation, even when you feel you have closed all your vulnerable openings. It is a fight you must be up for to maintain your stance and success. Fear cannot be run from, or it will steal the ground you have gained. So if you have allowed fear to rule and run your life, it is time that you have a talk with the fears in your life and let them know that God is in control, and there is no room for fear to live there anymore. So, give fear an eviction notice and put it out of your mind and heart. None of us are truly free until we allow God to master our lives and our fate. He allows us to be the captain of our ship knowing God moves the ocean, and our times are in His hands. I want to introduce you to Zaire.

On the surface, Zaire is a strong, outgoing, intelligent, and athletic young man. He has advanced degrees as well as a license for counseling. I was drawn to him because of his sincere desire to fit in and to be part of a passionate group. We began to work together and as we talked and became more acquainted, I found that his conversation was laced with fears of being accepted. He explained that he wanted to be involved but was convinced most people wouldn't accept him. "They never have," he said. He continued to explain that his decisions are usually based on those feelings. Since we were alone and could take time to talk, I inquired about relationships. Zaire shared how he has been in several serious relationships but because of his fears, he either ran them off or shut it down because he feared being left and rejected, like his parents left and rejected him. I asked Zaire if we could sit down and talk further about this issue and perhaps find the root of it and destroy it at the root. He was more than willing to meet and stated he hoped I would take time to speak with him.

At our next meeting, Zaire began by describing himself as someone who doesn't have an original thought because of not wanting people to reject him. So, he normally waits for others to suggest things and jumps on board with them. He calls himself a people watcher, not to learn from them but to copy them. Like countless others he values their behavior, acts, conversations, and style greater than his own. He believes he acclimates to the behaviors of others because it's just easier to fit in and to be accepted. Zaire describes himself as young as three to five years old being sent to live with his grandparents, because his parents were getting a divorce and he overheard them yelling at each other that the other parent needed to be responsible for him. The final analysis was that neither one wanted him! The event told his young mind he didn't matter. It was the beginning of Zaire dealing with the feelings of being rejected. Although his grandparents had a stable home, he never felt good enough. They withheld love when he misbehaved and compared him to others so harshly that he began to copy those people to make them happy. Now there is nothing wrong with modeling other people or their behavior. All of us do this from time to time, but there is a big difference between modeling others' behavior and making their behavior your own out of fear of rejection. The basis of modeling is to improve yourself or your livelihood. It's important not to lose yourself in modeling others. The first thing is making sure it's not done out of fear. Zaire struggled as a young boy for acceptance; he has lost all sense of identity. Zaire's personal identity, and his personal brand, must be restored so that he can live in a healthy emotional place.

Zaire realized his fear of rejection caused him to appear needy to others, and it may have contributed to the demise of his relationships, since most of his life he watched and gathered ideas, thoughts, and behaviors from others caused him to tend to be very needy. Zaire needed people to make him feel happy. He craved their attention to feel whole, and because he sought their approval, he found it extremely difficult to say no! Since the fear of rejection parades itself through your life and is easily seen, other people can sense that you are needy, and that you seek constant approval. As a result, they will either manipulate you for their own purposes, or they will just literally take you for granted. Either way, you lose. People are naturally drawn and want to associate with others who are confident. They want to be with people who value their own worth by knowing they matter. These are the type of people that all of us should model. They are rarely manipulated or taken for granted because they walk in the confidence that they matter. Zaire admitted living most of his life to this day in extreme dissatisfaction and guilt about everything he has tried to accomplish. He explained that even gaining degrees, or knowing he did the work, he still did not feel good enough. Zaire says he has never been truly happy. I understood his statement because happiness comes from within. But Zaire built his feelings on what others do, say, or think. This all goes back to the little boy who received the spirit of rejection at five years old and lost a measure of his self-esteem. Sometimes a lack of self-confidence stems from not having a sense of accomplishment. Even after all Zaire has accomplished in his life, he still feels he has not achieved anything of significance in this world. Because of these feelings, it pushes Zaire to look to others for cues of what he should or shouldn't do in most situations.

Zaire's introduction to the spirit of rejection that brought fear with it, stems from the fact that he was constantly being compared to others, which convinced him that he must now imitate other people's behavior, values, beliefs, opinions and more, just to be accepted. Since Zaire was able to pinpoint when or where the root began, we were able to create steps toward healing. The first step is to figure out what you really want. What do you want for your life? Then it is important to explore the reason why. You must dig deep to find reasons that have nothing to do with what others think. It needs to be legitimate reasons that you can build the best years of your life on. Part of finding your why is looking at why this is important to you to accomplish the healing you need. Once you have found the why, next is to determine how you will benefit from what you want; how will it change your past and impact your future? What are you looking forward to doing or becoming? Finally, what will happen if you fail to overcome and heal from your fear of rejection? All of this is step one; take time to make your answers meaningful. The next step is to gain clear vision. This means to look at what it is exactly you fear! To get to that, there are a few questions you can ask yourself. For example, what type of rejection am I afraid of? Whose rejection do I fear the most? Ask yourself, how do I behave when I fear being rejected? How does this behavior hinder me? How is it hurting me? Now that you have identified the type of fear and the negative behavior, it's time to build positive responses to the negativity you have lived with. Begin with thinking about a situation in which you may experience the fear of rejection.

Ask yourself, how else can I approach this situation? How can I think differently about this situation? How can these changes be helpful? Give yourself time to think through all obstacles that you might need to work through in order to fully embrace your newly-found freedom. Name potential obstacles standing in the way of your freedom. Are they real or imagined? What steps can I prepare to overcome these obstacles, both real and imagined? When it comes to the fear of rejection, many of the obstacles you face are only in your head. And because they are in your head, you can most certainly overcome them, if you're honest with yourself and committed to making a change for the better. Finally, this is not a microwave process. You must commit to ongoing daily self-improvement. These are the bricks and mortar of pulling your life together and building your self-esteem over time. The passage of time should help you build social skills. We live in a social world and risk interacting daily with other social beings. During some of these interactions, you may be criticized, judged, and rejected. It's unavoidable; all of us must prepare for these encounters. Even though you can't control what other people will think or do, you can; however, minimize the likelihood and the impact that rejection has on you by developing your social skills and your ability to assert yourself when required. The more you work through this process the more confidence you will have within yourself. After a while of positive movement, you will see others trying to model you and your behavior instead of the other way around.

The Green-Eyed Monster (Envy)

As much as we want to believe and think we feel genuinely happy for friends and family when they get that special thing, we must admit the chill of jealousy and envy has blown past our ears and disturbed us. The Bible illustrates many stories of people fighting through these types of issues. Looking at the story, we learn that it's impossible to defeat jealousy and envy without dealing with our own personal disappointment and pain. That type of pain only God has the power to take away. Let's peek at David's story to understand the importance of dealing with disappointments and let downs so they don't become the root of your envy tree. There are times in our lives when nothing seems to go according to plan. Sometimes it feels like every effort you make is either rejected, misunderstood or just not good enough. There are people who cannot deal with any kind of disappointment, so they react as though life is no longer worth living. In these times, you may feel like withdrawing, giving up and throwing in the towel. God wants us to be victorious over every situation and circumstance, especially over those that cause us to be downcast. It seems strange, but God works all situations for our good, yes! All of them, the good, the bad, the ugly and the sad, He has a way of stirring them together so that what comes out is nothing but good for you and me. There is a lesson to learn even when we feel the rug has been pulled from under us. David learned that all good ideas are not God ideas!

This is empowering because no matter how people may treat us or what things we may not have in life, we can always be satisfied and confident if we are friends with God. David loved the Lord, and so wanted to do something big to honor and thank Him for the abundant blessings he had received. David's relationship with God was one of friendship and father love. He had seen the way the Lord had worked in his life since the day he was called. Through God, David caused Goliath and the Philistines to be defeated. This single-handed victory caused the kingdom to be secure. David was blessed by God to live in a beautiful palace, but his heart was heavy because the Ark of the Covenant was in a tent in Jerusalem. People who have the heart of God always want the people and things of God to be great!

> *"So they brought the ark of God, and set it in the midst of the tent that David had pitched for it: and they offered burnt sacrifices and peace offerings before God."*
> — *(1 Chronicles 16:1)*

This grieved David so much that he made plans to erect a temple for God. To everyone hearing his plan it sounded great; even David felt his plan was good. His thoughts were that God deserved more than a tent. David thought if a wonderful temple could be built for God, it would prove to Israel and the surrounding nations that the Lord was truly worshipped and honored by His people. David's plan did not come from his head but from his heart. In our lives today, we would probably want to do more for God if we sat down and counted the many blessings He has brought into our lives. Even the prophet Nathan backed David's plan when he told him what he wanted to do. The entire nation of Israel had to feel great that their king wanted to honor the Lord in this way. While everyone was thrilled about David's plan, no one consulted God. Remember, a good plan, a heart plan, a love plan may not be God's plan! God's ways are far above our ways. He is strategic in all His plans; everything is within His control and for a future hope of mankind! When Nathan went to pray and talk to God, he was set straight by God for not consulting Him first. It has been said, "What man proposes, God disposes," which means "People can make plans; God determines how things will turn out." (*The New Dictionary of Cultural Literacy*) Nathan had to tell David that God did not want him to build a temple. David had to feel the ultimate rejection, not only of his plan but also of himself as well. God spoke to David's heart and he soon understood why God had not permitted him to build the temple. If God says no, it may be because He has a better plan than ours. It is interesting to note that instead of David building a house for God, God built a house for David that would last forever. Prophetically, this is known as the Davidic Covenant, which finds its fulfilment in the Lord Jesus Christ. (Matthew 1:1, 22:42)

Dealing with Your Jealousy

The Bible says in the book of Solomon, jealousy is crueler than the grave. (Solomon 8:6) James takes it a little bit further, *"But if you have bitter jealousy and selfish ambition in your hearts, do not boast and be false to the truth."* (James 3:14, *ESV*) When we discuss jealousy, we think about other folk's stuff, someone's car, house, possessions. Jealousy can be about anything! It can involve any combination of things and become very complicated. Then how do we overcome this issue? That's a great question. Jealousy is not easy to overcome but all things are possible through Jesus Christ. You can overcome jealousy and become all that God has designed you to be!

The danger of jealousy is a spiritual issue. Its ability to cripple people is so strong that God penned in the 10th Commandment, *"Thou shalt not covet."* Jealousy is a form of covetousness. We find throughout the Bible, instructions on avoiding or overcoming this dreadful character trait of covetousness.

"Let your conduct be without covetousness; be content with such things as you have. For he Himself has said, "I will never leave you nor forsake you."
— (Hebrews 13:5, NKJV)

196

This chapter in Hebrews teaches us that when covetousness (jealousy) is present, it also brings its friends, discontent and lack of thankfulness. When we allow jealousy to run our lives, what we are saying is that what God provides is not enough, because He has given so much more to others! We start believing that God isn't really without respect of person! Our conduct indicates that we believe that God does have picks and chooses because look what he has! Look where he lives! It is important to know that jealousy can turn into a competition with anyone you feel jealous about. If you believe they have the best, the competition is on and crackin,' If you believe they are better, then it's on! You're in a whirlwind of struggle trying to pull yourself above the pettiness of jealousy. When we fall into pettiness and the spirit of jealousy has a strong hold on your heart, these attitudes are so pleasing to the god of this world which is Satan!

Now don't get me wrong, there is nothing wrong with wanting things and asking God to bless you with them. You have to end your request to God with your "amen," meaning into Your hands, God, I give my desires because I know You have already mapped out what's good for me and what I truly need to obtain my expected destiny. The Apostle Paul spoke often about being content. He in no way meant to be satisfied! But what he was saying was, use what's in your hand now to make room for what's coming to you in the future. Being content reminds us that the things we obtain in this life are temporal but what we seek and strive toward is the Kingdom of God, because it is what was, what is and what is to come, from everlasting to everlasting. So how can we overcome jealousy? Glad you asked!

We begin by going through an emotional inventory to identify the causes of your jealous thoughts. Begin by making a list of the things that bring on your feelings of jealousy. Once you have that list, start questioning those emotions with questions like:

- Am I happy? With me? With my life? With what I have gained?
- Why am I not happy for others?
- If I receive everything, I'm jealous about will I be happy then?
- Is it because what I see around me makes me feel I'm less-than? Where does that come from?
- Have I tied my happiness to things that are temporary?

Then begin to remind yourself that God loves you best and He wants only what's best for you. He will never give you what will harm you yesterday, today or in your future. The Bible tells us that all good gifts come from the Father of Lights, God Himself. Always remember that what we are jealous about rarely deals with what we need. For the most part, and most of the time, you are dealing with your wants. These wants come from the flesh, (your feelings), and not from the God of your spirit. We must constantly check our thoughts to ensure they don't begin to stink! Jealousy comes from a petty place such as harboring stinking thoughts like greed, laziness, being unthankful, ungrateful, ungodly, and being self-serving. So, let's do some personal surgery to get to the root of your feelings and emotions. These are undesirable attributes that breed a cancer of the spirit called jealousy. Cancers must be cut out! After these attributes have been eradicated, it's time for the ministry of replacement. They need to be replaced with life-giving words of affirmation that take root and grow into healing for wounded spirits. Start with thankfulness and blessings. Make a list of the things you're thankful for in your life, the triumphs you have enjoyed spiritually, physically, mentally and socially due to God smiling on you and your life. Begin to acknowledge God in every area of your life, the good and the bad, believing *"...all things God works for the good of those who love him, who have been called according to his purpose."* (Romans 8:28, *NIV*) Start watching how your attitude about stuff and what others have begins to change. Working to arrive at a place where you appreciate the gifts of God more than you want the stuff of Satan means you're on the road to controlling and destroying the spirit of jealousy.

Overcoming Depression

Sadly, the truth is many Christian men and women suffer from depression. Because it is such a difficult issue in the church, many suffer in silence, or they are unaware of the reasons they seem to be miserable most of the time. Admitting that you are suffering like this opens you up to being diagnosed by church folk who quickly decide you have a spiritual problem. So most choose the route of least resistance, suffering in silence hoping, praying, and seeking deliverance. The awful truth is, doing nothing can be the worst decision of all. It should be the endeavor of all who love the Lord to seek and work toward being comforters of all who suffer from any source. If we are going to accomplish this, we need to free our own minds from false assumptions and quick remedies by fully grasping the causes of depression, which allows the Holy Spirit to use you to

199

help others gain the victory. So, what is depression? According to the *Textbook of Natural_Medicine*, 2nd Edition, Joseph Pizzorno, ND & Michael Murray, ND, Bastyr University, the most common symptoms are:

- deep sadness or emptiness
- apathy, loss of interest or pleasure in usual activities
- agitation or restlessness, physical hyperactivity, or inactivity
- sleep disturbances
- weight/appetite disturbances
- diminished ability to think or concentrate
- feelings of excessive guilt, self-reproach, or worthlessness
- feelings of fatigue or loss of energy
- morbid thoughts of death or suicide

The textbook indicates that if a person has five (5) or more of these symptom experiences for a month, they have major depression. Mild depression is described by the same group as having two to four symptoms for a month. There are also the diagnoses of bipolar disorder or some may call it "manic depressive" can include cycles of deeply depressive moods to wildly manic moods. In speaking with women who suffer from depression, I've asked them, "Where do you find pleasure in life? Or, what in life brings you pleasure?"

Most look down at their feet and state, "I don't know," or they say, "Nothing." Saved (born again) depressed men want to be spiritual so they reply, "Knowing or working for Christ" or "Knowing He loves me." Although saved, depressed people know they are afforded the eternal blessings from God and Heaven, they are deeply grateful while at the same time feeling locked down and trapped with inescapable emotional explosions and moods. A famous depressed man described his depression like this:

> *"I am now the most miserable man living. If what I feel were equally distributed to the whole human family, there would be not one cheerful face on earth. Whether I shall ever be better I cannot tell; I awfully (regretfully) forebode (foretell) I shall not. To remain as I am is impossible; I must die or be better, it appears to me."*
> —*Abraham Lincoln*

Experiences like this keep great people from pursuing all that God has created them to be, or their lives are cut short by reason of the torment they try to live through. These types of feelings may come from a moment of sadness, that moment grows into ongoing grief. If this grief is left unchecked, it can lead down the rabbit hole to depression. There is a famous woman who seemed to have symptoms of depression and that was Hannah. (1 Samuel 1) It is an excellent example of spiritual leadership getting it wrong by instantly diagnosing her as having a spiritual problem. We in the church who do not suffer with depression, and especially our leaders, rarely understand the ongoing, unrelenting pain and the feelings of hopelessness these precious folks endure. Many of us are guilty of thinking, as well as preaching and sharing messages, that these people should just pick themselves up and get over it! The truth is that when the part of the brain that regulates emotions is off balance, its medical help that's needed, not condemnation and innuendos. An article I remember reading indicated an estimation of ten million people in the United States suffer from depression. It has also been stated that older Christians are diagnosed in ever increasing numbers with depression. Would we say God does not or cannot keep your mind if you keep it on Him? To the contrary, living in this dying world causes us who are aging to have more biochemical and brain malfunctions as we age, and depression is a natural consequence. Within that number, women stand out as being diagnosed with depression two to three times more than men. Be clear that we are not saying women have more spiritual problems than men. However, we do process events and especially adverse events differently, due to our complex body chemistry that naturally gets off balance monthly, which can lead to depression if the off balance falls outside of normal boundaries. Women tend to be more sensitive than their male counterparts, internalizing issues more readily and tending to accept blame easier. I certainly don't want to minimize this devastating issue or act as if I can easily diagnose the problem, but I encourage you to seek medical help if you find yourself described within these pages. When we seek to understand the causes of depression, what we run into is an exhaustive list of possible agents, and what we see if several of these agents are at work at the same time. Let's look at some things known to contribute to depression.

- nutrient deficiency or excess
- drugs (prescription, illicit, caffeine)
- hypoglycemia (low blood sugar)
- hormonal imbalances
- allergies
- heavy metals
- sexual abuse as a child
- microbial overgrowths/toxins

- medical conditions (stroke, heart disease, cancer, Parkinson's, diabetes, thyroid)
- natural light deprivation
- psychological factors (generally poor thought-processing)
- spiritual factors

The Bible tells us that if we are going to be agents of change, agents of help and agents of support, we must do what 2 Corinthians 1:6, 7 tell us:

> "When we suffer for Jesus, it works out for your healing and salvation. If we are treated well, given a helping hand and encouraging word, that also works to your benefit, spurring you on, face forward, unflinching. Your hard times are also our hard times. When we see that you're just as willing to endure the hard times as to enjoy the good times, we know you're going to make it, no doubt about it."
> — (2 Corinthians 1:6, 7 MSG)

The unwanted attack of this enemy of your health can fight your body, soul, and spirit, one at a time or all at once. Remember, something attacking your spirit does not imply a change in your status or position in Christ. Some recent research beginning in 1990 revealed that most depressed people have a decrease in the frontal lobes' blood flow and activity, which is believed to be involved in emotional well-being. The same type of research indicated that depressed children have significantly smaller frontal lobes than non-depressed children. Just as fog on a California shore clouds your ocean view, so depression clouds life itself. There are things that can be done to break through the fog of darkness bringing back sunny days. In this writing, I would like to suggest a combination of help and support, to assist those suffering from this disease and issue, to feel more normal and equip them with the ability to control their own minds through the power and anointing of the Holy Spirit.

The *Textbook of Natural Medicine* shares that herbs can be considered medicine from God's pharmacy! The advantages of herbal supplements are that they can often effect a cure rather than just addressing symptoms, with minor side effects. When considering herbs as one of the steps toward recovery, consider these tested herbs:

- St. John's Wort (SJW): relieves depression, anxiety, apathy, sleep disturbance, anorexia, and feelings of worthlessness. All these symptoms are caused by low serotonin and SJW increases the level of serotonin in the brain.
- Ginkgo biloba: improves blood flow and function of the frontal lobes. Ginkgo increases the ability of serotonin to do its job in the brain.
- 5-HTP: a plant extract that is just one step from becoming serotonin—the brain readily makes this conversion. It raises the level of serotonin and other brain neurotransmitters. This product overcomes the genetic problem that does not allow for the conversion of tryptophan to 5-HTP.

Although I believe if the natural way works for you, it is the way to go, I do not want to leave you feeling it is the only way. Doctor-ordered medication can save your life. Just like any other disease, if a lifestyle change does not bring about optimum results, then your doctor's prescription for medication is your best choice. Antidepressant drugs may be just what you need in order to function well. Speak with your doctor about both prescription medications and botanical medications. Along with nutrition, one or both may be the answer. Remember, the rule of thumb from a biblical perspective is to consume foods that have a mother, are grown from the earth and are available as close to the way God created them as possible. Pay attention to purchasing whole, raw, and unprocessed foods. It was never God's intention for us to consume processed foods or animal meat that's full of antibiotics and hormones that adversely affect our bodies natural functions. The way God has designed our bodies, we are best fed on the whole foods He has designed.

Stressors

It is so important that we have God's view of the world. His view is never for us to feel like victims. God's design is for us to know that He is working in our lives and has ordered our steps. He has told us to choose positive thoughts. In Philippians 4:8, 9, *The Message Bible,* it says:

> "Summing it all up, friends, I'd say you'll do best by filling your minds and meditating on things true, noble, reputable, authentic, compelling, gracious—the best, not the worst; the beautiful, not the ugly; things to praise, not things to curse. Put into practice what you learned from me, what you heard and saw and realized. Do that, and God, who makes everything work together, will work you into his most excellent harmonies."

Our thought life drives all that we say and do. It determines our temperament, sound thoughts, sound actions and behavior. Our world becomes a better place when we think on the things God has determined. This does not mean that bad, or worse, or even ugly things won't happen to you. As a matter of fact, they will happen at some time in your life. You may lose a job, or a family member. People may do things that disappoint or hurt you, but the Bible says God will make everything work together, and not only that, God will make the good and the bad things become harmony, excellent harmony in your life. Negative thoughts destroy all the work you have done through nutrition, herbs, and medication. These thoughts undermine your destiny while destroying your health.

They must be brought under the subjection of the Holy Spirit. It is so important that we resist contemplating on negative things. We need to give special effort in guarding our hearts from negative people. It is our duty and our charge as much as it is our privilege to pray daily. God's world has so many awesome and wonderful things as well as beautiful sights to see. There are people only involved in making the lives of others better by giving and providing for their needs. Being involved or contributing to groups like this gives you a better outlook and thought on life. It will improve your entire outlook. Thinking on these things is our charge and to do this takes practice. Most of us have entertained negative thoughts for years and you will need to practice the art of replacement thought. Every time you think on negative things, you immediately replace it with either positive thoughts or Scripture. The Bible tells us to bring all our thoughts into captivity to the obedience of Christ. (2 Corinthians 10:5) In other words, do not allow your thoughts to run wild, but control your own mind and what you allow it to do. Even if the negative thoughts are true, or if it is something someone has done to you, make sure you do not allow these thoughts to keep running over and over again in your mind. If you do, they have a tendency to take over your entire thought life.

Life and Death Matters

You never want to live in a place of ignorance concerning life or death. Both extremes of life take planning and management. Positioning yourself to be secure in life and death should be at the core of every Christian's thoughts, desires, and plans. The importance of knowing your financial reality must become part of the forefront of your plans for the security of yourself and your family. Managing your finances means putting demands on your money that includes a plan for increasing those resources. These demands include gaining knowledge and alliances that promote the practice of managing your money. I really understand that taking a hard look at finances can be like watching the latest horror/slasher movie. Although you may be scared out of your wits, you continue to look, peeking through parted fingers covering your eyes, hoping to miss the goriest parts. This too is how many of us approach our financial habits, preferring not to look, as if it's not real if you don't see it. The reality is, you must open your eyes even though you hate what's happening in your financial life. The promises of the Bible are always associated with a premise. God has said you can have what I promise if you do what I say! Many have practiced good standards, as it pertains to giving to the work of the Lord, through tithes and offerings, as if just by practicing good things and living in a good way will make everything alright. Being a good *steward* means, "Utilizing and managing all resources God provides for the glory of God and the betterment of His creation," according to *Wikipedia.org.* Deuteronomy 28:1-6 puts it this way:

> *"Carefully obey the LORD your God, and faithfully follow all his commands that I'm giving you today. If you do, the Lord your God will place you high above all the other nations in the world. These are all the blessings that will come to you and stay close to you because you OBEY the LORD your God:*
>
> *You will be blessed in the city and blessed the country.*
>
> *You will be blessed. You will have children. Your land will have crops. Your animals will have offspring. Your cattle will have calves, and your flocks will have lambs and kids.*
>
> *The grain you harvest and the bread you bake will be blessed.*
>
> *You will be blessed when you come and blessed when you go."*
> *— (GOD'S WORD Translation, GW)*

God is faithful to us if we are faithful to His premises. We are not able to grow anything if we do not follow how the seed should be planted, and what it will require for it to increase in size and yield abundance. God is promising blessings in your personal life, family life and your world. These promises hinge on the premise of obedience to the premises associated with the type of blessing you receive. There are natural laws for things on Earth to produce a great harvest. In the same way, there are spiritual laws for blessings to produce abundance in your life. When fear grips your very being, take the necessary steps to overthrow it immediately. First, pray about it. Make your requests known to God by going boldly before His throne. Realize that you are the daughter or son of God. Two, cultivate right-thinking by disciplining your mind with positive thoughts. This will prevent you from falling prey to the tricks of the devil. Three, meditate on God's Word and regain your stance of faith. Then manage your reactions and responses. This step will usher you into the peace that only God can provide.

If your life now or in times past has been plagued by fear, it is time that you face it once and for all. Stand up and give fear an eviction notice. Put it out of your heart and mind and begin to live victoriously in the power of God and His love everlasting!

CHAPTER ELEVEN

FROM DUNGAREES TO DIAMONDS:

Unconquerable and Indestructible

―――――――――――― ༄ ― ――――――――――――

According to the *Oxford Dictionary*, the definition of a *jewel* is, "A precious stone, typically a single crystal or piece of a hard lustrous or translucent mineral ..." One of the most precious stones known to man is the diamond. The Greek word for diamond is *adamas* which means "unconquerable or indestructible." In 327 BC, Alexander the Great brought the first diamond to Europe from India, the land where diamonds were first discovered. Romans believed that diamonds had power to ward off evil spirits and wore them as talismans. In 1477, Mary of Burgundy received a diamond engagement ring from Archduke Maximilian of Austria. As a result, the history and tradition of the diamond engagement ring continues to this day.

The largest diamond, the Cullinan, was discovered in 1905 and weighed in at 3,106.75 carats. It was named after Thomas Cullinan, chairman of the Premier Mine in South Africa. Its nickname is the Great Star of Africa. The Crater of Diamonds State Park in Arkansas is the world's only diamond mine open to the public where one can experience a dig-free operation for tourists and rock enthusiasts. A diamond nicknamed "Uncle Sam" was found there in 1924.

The diamond is the hardest of all gemstones known to man. It is also the simplest in composition and is made up of only one element—common carbon. Approximately 250 tons of ore must be mined and processed from the average Kimberlite pipe to produce a one-carat polished diamond of gem quality. Kimberlite is the name given to volcanic rock.

Diamonds are carried to the Earth's surface by volcanic eruptions. Very few diamonds survive the hazardous journey from the depths of the Earth to its surface. Diamonds are brittle; if hit hard with a hammer, a diamond will shatter or splinter. Even though a diamond can be broken, a diamond seemingly lasts forever.

In contrast, dungarees are worn as casual clothing. The value of dungarees does not compare to that of a diamond. For this discussion, dungarees represent the basics of who we are, or the struggles of trying to become who God has called us to be. It's a heavy material, like many of the things in our lives that weigh us down. Diamonds, on the other hand, represent who we become as we go through the trials and tribulations in our lives. The trials and tribulations can be likened to violent, hot, and disruptive volcanic activity that produces the rarest of stones, known as the diamond.

Although you started this journey as a diamond in the rough, your value was not readily apparent. You may have been overlooked and picked over. It took time for the dirt and rough edges to wear off, but God spoke over your life and called you a diamond when others only considered you insignificant. What other people did not know was that diamonds that have been cut, polished, and touched by too many hands lose their value. God held you and kept you for a time such as this! It has always been His plan to bring you from the background into the forefront. People will look at you and wonder why you were chosen and why you matter! They will only see your flaws and the dirt from the mountains you survived.

Many of your flaws were formed from the pressures of the mountains you endured. You thought you needed to be shiny for your brilliance to matter. But the truth is, a rough diamond is the purest and most natural form of diamond there is because it has not yet been polished or perfected. God has chosen you for your uniqueness, your special qualities, and your flaws, which add value and strength to who you are.

Be careful not to blend in with the crowd. They chase what's in fashion, which causes a fluctuation in value. Rough diamonds have the advantage of never "going out of style." God never intended for you to tailor yourself after others. His Word tells us not to conform to this world, but to be transformed by the renewing of our minds. This implies changing your thought patterns from conforming to transformational. *"And do not be conformed to this world, but be transformed by the renewing of your mind, that you may prove what is that good and acceptable and perfect will of God."* (Romans 12:2, *NKJV*)

In the original Greek language of the New Testament, the word used for *transformation* is *metamorphosis.* The biological definition for metamorphosis, according to *www.dictionary.com,* is, "a profound change in form from one stage to the next in the life history of an organism, as from the caterpillar to the pupa and from the pupa to the adult butterfly." Although an outward change in appearance takes place, the change comes from within the life of the organism. A caterpillar is born to become a butterfly, just as you were born again to become a refined diamond. The caterpillar doesn't put on a butterfly costume or strive to act like a butterfly. The nutrients it consumes and assimilates causes it to become a real, genuine butterfly.

A caterpillar's transformation into a butterfly is an excellent example of what the Bible speaks of concerning the believer's transformation into the image of Christ. Finding our place in Him is what matters above everything. Transformation takes time, and as children of the Most-High God, we must consume the Word to nourish our spirit. This process causes our spiritual

metabolism to grow, as we continue to develop into valuable lifelong diamonds in Him!

The following list was taken from *Bibles for America*.org. It states that calling on the name of Jesus throughout the day and telling Him how much we love Him facilitates our transformation. The Word of God is our daily bread. In addition:

- We should sing with our spirit to the Lord.
- We should pray with our spirit.
- We should pray over what we read in the Bible.

- We should give thanks to God.
- We should praise God.
- We should preach the Gospel or speak about Christ to others.

Becoming a Diamond King

Although you may have endured great pressure, contradiction and misinformation during your life, it's time for you to get rid of the mental mirror that reminds you of things that have hindered you in the past. Give the king in you permission to outshine your past. It doesn't matter what your size, shape, color or circumstances may be. You were created to be not only a king, but a *diamond king*. A king is a man who has a royal place, but a diamond king creates his place based on his ability to overcome issues that would have taken a lesser man out. He shines through the hardest dirt. Start telling yourself the truth today! Say this out loud right now: "I am perfect for my purpose. I was fearfully, carefully, skillfully and wonderfully created."

If anyone calls on you because of your remarkable talent or skill, answer the call! There is no better person to fulfil the request than you! You are truly a remarkable man, and it's high time you acknowledge that fact. Diamonds in the raw hold great value, but they are difficult to recognize by the untrained eye. It is nearly impossible to mount an uncut diamond. However, you were created to be mounted, crowned, and put on display because you are a *diamond king*.

You may have thought you lost something because of the circumstances you have faced, but the cuts of life are bringing forth great brilliance in you. Don't be mistaken; cuts are not blemishes. They have come to make you strong. Cuts allow rays of light to flow through the many facets of your life, displaying your beauty. All of us are at different stages in our lives. For example, I may have endured a simple cut, which forms its own beauty. On the other hand, you may have a multifaceted cut, which allows a greater amount of light to flow through.

Each cut was handled by the Skilled Jeweler, Who knows the intended outcome. However, appreciation of who you are must begin within you. This level of appreciation-shift begins with renewing your mind and once and for all resolving the conflict over who you are and what your talent and purpose is in life. Let's review a few points to help you settle into your kingdom, dear king:

Practice Mindfulness - the practice of maintaining a nonjudgmental state of heightened or complete awareness of one's thoughts, emotions, or experiences on a moment-to-moment basis (*Merriam-Webster.com*). To practice this art, there are components we must include in our practice. Being mindful means making peace with who you are and coming to grips with what is most important to you. Don't worry; take a deep breath and dive in headfirst. You will receive great satisfaction from bringing this practice into your daily routine.

- Awareness – To begin this practice, pay attention to you, and only you. This means you must establish time in each day to simply be quiet. Whether that is 5, 10, 15 minutes or more, make that time for yourself to assess where you are in the day and address what you are feeling and experiencing in present tense. Turn off the phone, TV, music, and anything else that demands your attention and pulls your mind away from you. If you have family – children, spouse, others – communicate your need to have this time and take it without guilt. Quietly notice your thoughts, feelings, and physical sensations as they happen. Your goal isn't to clear your mind or to stop thinking. It is to become more aware of your thoughts and feelings. This awareness does not mean getting lost in thoughts or emotions. It means hearing them, feeling them, and recognizing them as your own.

- Acceptance – This may be difficult for those who have dealt with criticism and those who may be uncomfortable with their own thoughts and feelings. I am asking you to dismiss any old, outdated thoughts that may have hindered you or tried to shame you in some way in the past. Begin acknowledging your feelings, thoughts, and sensations in a nonjudgmental manner. As you notice thoughts, feelings, and sensations, acknowledge them as yours. For example, if you are feeling nervous, just say to yourself, "I notice I am feeling nervous." Don't feel pressure to change the feeling or thought. Just acknowledge that it is there. The Bible teaches us that God is mindful of us, and He notices everything we do. The Scriptures tell us that not even a small bird can fall to the ground without God knowing.

There is no one who cares more about you than God does. He is fully aware of whatever concerns you, worries you, causes you fear or keeps you up at night. He knows you well and best. God cares for you and He is perfecting everything that concerns you. Because God is alert and focused on you, you should be alert and focused on your thoughts as well. Mindfulness will help guide you to your purpose and provide direction for your destiny. To practice this art form, consider mindful meditation and mindful walking.

Mindful Meditation

- Meditation: the revolving around and around in the mind of something of great
- importance: turning a subject over and over until one is talking or murmuring to oneself about it; to utter, imagine, pray, speak. (*Merriam-Webster.com*)

- Ponder: to weigh something in the mind until all barriers that stand in the way of
- understanding it fully have been removed; is used to describe the rolling or flattening of bumpy ground to make it into a roadway. (*Merriam-Webster.com*)

- Consider: to see, understand by looking long at a problem; to return again and again to the subject; to note carefully, to fully observe, to behold, and, in beholding, discover. (*Merriam-Webster.com*)

We must learn to think what our hearts already know, for it is our thoughts that produce our lifestyles. What we are in our thoughts about today will determine the way we live tomorrow. The Bible teaches us to renew our minds by transforming our thoughts by reading and meditating on God's Word. We can only do that by studying God's Word and believing in our heart what we read.

As you practice mindfulness, you will learn more about yourself. You're probably thinking, *"I already know myself."* Most people feel that way, but this practice helps us to identify more clearly who we are. You must believe in the good in your heart, which God has placed inside you. Begin by sitting in a comfortable place, hearing and feeling your breathing. Notice the physical sensation of air filling your lungs and the release of air out of your nostrils. When your mind wanders and it will, simply pay attention to your thoughts at that moment and return to your breathing. Do this for several minutes until you feel a sense of calm and awareness of the rhythm of your breathing. Read or recite Scriptures or words of affirmation in your mind that encourage and uplift your soul.

Mindful Walking

A king must always be aware of his steps to ensure that they are ordered by the Lord. Being mindful while walking means to become very aware of your walk. Notice how your body moves and feels with each step you take. This will tell you where your stressors are and if your steps are even and rhythmic. Then, take in your surroundings; use your senses to speak to your mind. What do you see? Colors? Shapes? Textures? What do you hear? Birds? Dogs? Wind? What do you smell? Flowers? Grass? Trees? What do you feel? Heat? Free? Love? Anxiety?

As you become mindful of yourself and your surroundings, begin to put a demand on your walk. Bring peace in your steps, love in every breath and wholeness as you move toward your desired direction. Practice this level of mindfulness until it becomes part of your daily routine. When things enter a king's atmosphere, trying to create drama, problems, or issues, he exercises his God-given authority to change his atmosphere and watch things move on his behalf.

God has prepared for us abundant life, and this life must be lived moment by moment, while being keenly aware of our surroundings. Determine to experience everything God has for you more deeply by experiencing it through your senses first – seeing, feeling, hearing, tasting, and smelling. Then experience it in your spirit through the power of the Holy Spirit, through the love of God, and with a sound mind. These gateways produce within you the fullness of the abundant life God has in mind for you and will empower you to minister to others, loving them as you love yourself.

Only out of the abundance of love that you have for yourself can you express agape love toward others. When you finally embrace you and the king within you, without condemnation and judgment, you will begin to freely express the strong light God designed you to be. You are on the road to walking in your destiny of peace, strength, love, and harmony, just as God intended.

Many men are totally unaware of themselves, their surroundings, and their true power. If you are one of them and you have been living life as it comes – without expectation and without putting a demand on your day – you are not living like the king you were designed to be. Don't allow abundant life to pass you by! You must seize this moment to ascertain the depth of your royalty. To seize the moment, you must push harder and reach further than you ever have before. You must take the blinders off and see your victories as gifts from God and your failures as preparation for greater things. No failure, guilt or problems can stop you when you are mindful of what's happening in your life.

Practice giving God all the glory through meditation. Thank Him in advance for your victories. This simple act will command a multitude of blessings to pour into your life. The Bible says God will keep your mind in perfect peace if you are mindful of Him. In the natural, it will reduce symptoms of depression, stress and anxiety and improve your memory and ability to focus. It will also improve your ability to adapt and manage emotions, especially in stressful situations. Meditation accompanied by praise will also make you keenly aware that God is in everything, transcending time and generations, everywhere, always. This awareness changes how you see everything, pushing you to make that extra step, knowing you're almost at your goal. Finishing any way other than strong is unacceptable.

CONCLUSION

This book is a call to action that begins in your spirit. It is a small flame that should ignite a fire that will burn through every fiber of your being! You not only matter to me, more importantly, you matter to God. Let this assurance empower you to move to the next level of abundant life.

The truths you have uncovered in these pages will help you take inventory of your life. Further, it will give you the power to scrutinize anything and anybody who is not striving for greater, reaching for more, and seeking God's highest. There will be those who will attempt to discourage you. Expect it! Perhaps the hardest thing to overcome will be the discouragement you will receive from those you love, trust, and admire.

It is at that time that you must refuse to give up. When these moments come, and they will, take time to remember why you decided to pursue your dream in the first place. When you find that place, replay it in your mind, hold it in your heart, and rekindle it in your spirit. It is in these difficult situations that mindfulness works best. Remain confident and stay connected to the truths found in God's Word. This will revive your dream and cause it to breathe again.

Now that you realize how much you matter to God; it should become easier to let go of the opinions others have of you. It may take time for this to become actualized in your spirit but keep at it. It is the negative thoughts, ideas and dreams of our past that attempt to hold power over us, when we allow them. However, when the truth is embraced, you can successfully do as Paul did: forget those things which are behind and press toward the mark of a higher calling. (Philippians 3:13, 14) This, my dear son and king, is freedom!

Your freedom in Christ is neither a pipe dream nor a daydream. This reality has rested on many kings before you. The dream God has given you is bigger than what you have imagined. It is a God-sized dream that should replace all the failed dreams your mind has rehearsed over time. Protect it with all your heart and don't allow fear to paralyze your efforts. If your steps are ordered by the Lord, He will see you through. Lean and depend on Him because through Him, you can do *all* things!

The act of renewing your mind to receive what God originally intended for your life will energize your resolve in everything you set your mind to do. This seed of truth gives endless possibilities to a life without walls or barriers, a life free from the bondage of this world and the people who are bound by it. You will be free to express your God-given talents and abilities whenever and wherever He leads.

As a diamond king, you have been called and anointed by God. Walk in this power; it will restore your self-worth and accelerate your purpose! It also allows God to breathe into you the grace to be the dad you want to be, the entrepreneur you're working to be, and the leader you were born to be. Don't fall into the trap of comparing yourself to others. Your outcome may seem the same as others, but your path is unique to you, your desires, and experiences. Never try to make your life-peg fit into someone else's life-hole. It will not fit.

Great men seek great counsel! They seek other men with proven records of trial, error, and most importantly, success. As you travel this transforming journey, seek those who will walk with you and fight for you. You do not need anyone in your inner circle who will help you make excuses or pull you into a downward spiral along with them.

The people in your inner circle must be for you! This is the qualification required of friends, lovers, and others. If they fail this test, they should not be in your closest circle. Removing the dead weight found in some relationships will set your spirit free. You may find it difficult to let some people go because they feed your old self, but with the newness of your mind and the freedom of your spirit, you will soar to heights you could never reach with them. Let them go!

Today, you are stronger than you were before you started, so stay on the mountain peak, never settling for the ground. You are an eagle; you were made to love the leap and experience the thrill of soaring on strong wings. Although you may have endured the limitations of your thoughts or the negative words and abusive actions of others, by reading this book, you have learned to hate the confinement of the yard. Therefore, never lose your inbred heritage of soaring by lowering your standards.

No matter what you've gone through, *you matter!* No matter how hard it may seem, *you matter!* Even if you are in a struggle right now, it does not negate the fact that *you matter!* Claim it today. Shout it from the mountaintop! Make this your response to everyone who attempts to contradict you: *"Yes, I do matter!"*

WORKS CITED

Britannica. n.d. *www.britannica.com/biography/LeBron-James*. Accessed September 2020.

Cheltenham, Sonya. n.d. "Pastor." *Christianity Today* .

Gardner, Chris. 2020. *Wikipedia.* March 18. Accessed September 29, 2020.

Lisa Kyle, Ph.D. n.d. *Are You Struggling With Too Many Talent, Skills, Ideas? You May Have*

www.ingramcontent.com/pod-product-compliance
Lightning Source LLC
Chambersburg PA
CBHW071214090426
42736CB00014B/2818